What Is
Corporate
Governance?

What Is Corporate Governance?

JOHN L. COLLEY, JR.
JACQUELINE L. DOYLE
GEORGE W. LOGAN
WALLACE STETTINIUS

McGraw-Hill

New York Chicago San Francisco Lisbon
London Madrid Mexico City Milan New Delhi
San Juan Seoul Singapore Sydney Toronto

1 2 3 4 5 6 7 8 9 0 DOC/DOC 0 9 8 7 6 5 4

ISBN 0-07-144448-3

This publication is designed to provide accurate and authoritative information in regard to the subject matter covered. It is sold with the understanding that neither the author nor the publisher is engaged in rendering legal, accounting, or other professional service. If legal advice or other expert assistance is required, the services of a competent professional person should be sought.
   —From a Declaration of Principles jointly adopted by Committee of the American Bar Association and a Committee of Publishers.

McGraw-Hill books are available at special quantity discounts to use as premiums and sales promotions, or for use in corporate training programs. For more information, please write to the Director of Special Sales, McGraw-Hill Professional, Two Penn Plaza, New York, NY 10121-2298. Or contact your local bookstore.

Library of Congress Cataloging-in-Publication Data

What is corporate governance? / by John L. Colley, Jr.
   [et al.].—1st ed.
      p.   cm.—(McGraw-Hill executive MBA series)
   ISBN 0-07-144448-3 (pbk. : alk. paper)
   1. Corporate governance.   2. Corporate governance
—United States.   I. Colley, John L. II. Series.
HD2741.W48 2005
658.4'2—dc22

                                    2004016697

CONTENTS

ACKNOWLEDGMENTS

We are grateful to the University of Virginia, The Darden Graduate School of Business Administration, the Darden School Foundation, and the Batten Institute for their support of this project.

It is a great pleasure for us to acknowledge the support and assistance of a number of administrators, faculty colleagues, and students, without whose help this book could not have been completed. Dean Robert Harris of the Darden School, Associate Dean of the Faculty Jim Freeland, and the Darden School's Research Committee have been strong supporters of our effort. The Batten Institute, its former executive director, Robert Bruner, and its director of research, Sankaran Venkataraman, provided valuable support. We also wish to thank our faithful assistant, Barbara Richards, for her extensive contributions to this effort. We are pleased to acknowledge the contributions of Jeff Gill and Tom Farrell to sections of this book dealing with the legal obligations of directors.

We are grateful to our esteemed colleague Ed Freeman, who has broadened our thinking, especially regarding the integral role of ethics in corporate governance, and in so doing, contributed to the betterment of this project.

We also wish to recognize a number of current and former students who assisted with various aspects of the book. We especially recognize the contributions of Kristin Hampton, Christopher Ling, Allison Sewell Bridges, and Sandipan Panigrahi.

We are grateful to the many students at the Darden School who have studied with us over the years and the numerous professional colleagues who have shared governance experiences with us. We particularly and gratefully acknowledge the contributions of Warren Batts, who assisted us with the initiation of our course on Corporate Governance.

We would also like to thank our gracious colleagues at McGraw-Hill for their association and support. We are grateful to Laura Libretti for her superior, professional administrative support. We are especially indebted to Kelli Christiansen for her unparalleled responsiveness and professionalism, her consistently constructive contributions, and her ever-optimistic support.

Finally, we especially acknowledge the generous patience and support of our families, who are partners in all of our efforts.

John L. Colley, Jr.
Jacqueline L. Doyle
George W. Logan
Wallace Stettinius
Charlottesville, Virginia
September 1, 2004

What Is
Corporate
Governance?

CHAPTER 1

CORPORATE GOVERNANCE MAKES HEADLINES

INTRODUCTION

Frustrations with the performance of publicly traded corporations have abounded for decades. Since the turn of the millennium, though, a confluence of events has served to focus the public eye on the prominent topic of corporate governance and its crucial importance to the U.S. and world economies. Enron... Arthur Andersen... WorldCom... Adelphia... Tyco; these debacles and widely publicized scandals, on the heels of the bursting of the dot.com tech bubble (with improprieties of its own), created an atmosphere of doubt and distrust among the investing public. Confidence failed in the ability of investors to make "informed" decisions, and the markets on which stocks of public corporations were traded faltered.

A nervous public grew anxious about the prospect of business failures, job losses, and the severe decline of its savings invested in corporate stocks. Questions were raised as to whether the transgressions were confined to the ranks of a few renegades, or whether the wrongdoing was systemic.

In response, the media, government, and various regulatory boards widened the scope of their scrutiny beyond the offending corporations. In doing so, they brought the broader social institution of the governance of publicly traded corporations into the media spotlight. For most, this meant an examination of the functioning of the boards of directors.

This book is intended to help readers of all levels of business sophistication gain a current understanding of what corporate governance entails, particularly for businesses governed by the laws of the United States. Our primary focus will be the for-profit, publicly traded company, meaning firms that have issued stock that are traded on a public stock exchange, such as the New York Stock Exchange (NYSE) or NASDAQ. This book is not intended to be used as a substitute for the governing documents of any particular organization or for the laws and regulations under which an organization operates.

WHAT IS GOVERNANCE?

To begin a discussion of corporate governance, we should first explore the topic of governance in general. Briefly, governance refers to the act or process of governing. Obviously, governance has existed since the dawn of civilization. History tells us of the never-ending evolution of models of governance, with periods of advancement and enlightenment interspersed with those of retrenchment and at times, temporary darkness. Most recently, we have witnessed the widespread embracing of representative government, most commonly democracy by and for the people, which took hold in America in the late eighteenth century.

WHAT IS CORPORATE GOVERNANCE?

As democracy flourished in the United States, it created a context for the free-market economic system referred to as capitalism. In the early days of the Industrial Revolution, an unrestrained form of capitalism resulted in a very small number of people becoming very wealthy while most stayed poor. The greedy and unscrupulous Robber Barons of the time could not be trusted as they created great personal wealth at the expense of their customers, workers, and public shareholders. The political system responded to the situation with laws and regulations intended to limit the excesses and abuses of the free and unrestrained markets of the time. In the end, capitalism prevailed under the watchful eye of the federal and state governments. As we have noted, this vigilance continues today.

The success of capitalism created opportunities for businesses to grow larger. One driver of this growth was the opportunity for investors to unite their capital (money) to fund extensive projects and massive enterprises. These investors became owners of portions or shares of the businesses in which they invested, and have come to be known as shareholders. The larger businesses that were created could not be governed effectively by proprietors and partnerships for many reasons. Consequently, in the twentieth century, the publicly owned corporation emerged as the dominant legal form for business enterprises.

The corporation has three distinctive features that make it an attractive form for defining the legal entity of a business—its unlimited life, the limited liability of the owners, and the divisibility of ownership that permits transfer of ownership interests without disrupting the structure of the organization. Interestingly, these attributes are rooted in a Supreme Court opinion written by Chief Justice John Marshall in 1819.[1]

Today, the public corporation itself operates as a form of representative government. The owners (shareholders) elect directors as their representatives to manage the affairs of the business. The directors, who as a group are referred to as the board of directors, then delegate responsibility for actual operations to the Chief Executive Officer (CEO), whom they hire. The CEO is accountable to the board of directors, which, collectively and individually, is accountable to the shareholders. In addition to its role in selecting the CEO, the board also advises on and consents to the selection of businesses and strategies of the firm as well as oversees results. In sum, this system of authoritative direction, or government, is known as *corporate governance*.

GOVERNANCE MAKES A DIFFERENCE

The relative effectiveness of corporate governance has a profound effect on how well a business performs. We have observed that businesses that have prospered and remained prosperous are those that have found ways to govern their affairs effectively. Similarly, with companies that have performed poorly, it is common to track the problems to boards that have not effectively addressed the issues confronting their businesses. The governance model of a successful corporation typically includes the following characteristics:

- An effective board of directors that carries out its responsibilities with integrity and competence.
- A competent CEO hired by the board and given the authority to run the business.
- Selection by the CEO of a "good" business (or businesses) in which to operate with the board's advice and consent. This means a business in which the firm can compete effectively and profitably in an industry that is reasonably attractive. It also implies that the company has the skills and resources necessary for competitive success.
- A valid business concept created by the CEO and his or her management team, and, again, with the board's advice and consent. A business concept encompasses the definition of the customer(s) to

be served, the goods and/or services to be delivered, and the means or processes by which these goods and services will be delivered. A valid business concept is one that meets the needs of the customer in a superior and often unique way that will allow the firm to become and/or remain profitable.

- Appropriate implementation of the business concept, which normally requires that:
  - There are broad goals that set the direction for the organization.
  - The CEO has plans and resources to achieve the organization's goals, and effectively executes the plans.
  - The interests of the board and management are aligned with those of the shareholders.
- Systems to ensure that the organization's obligations to its major stakeholders—customers, employees, creditors, suppliers and distributors, the community, and owners—are met with integrity and in compliance with applicable laws and regulations.
- Full and timely disclosure of the performance of the business to its owners and to the investment community at large.

A board of directors that fails to guarantee that a sound governance model is in place and executed conscientiously and effectively invites the failure of the enterprise it oversees. It is important to remember, however, that success is not just a matter of conforming to the legalities of corporate governance. Equally important to success is the creation and effective execution of a valid business concept.

THE STAKEHOLDER CONCEPT

The test of effectiveness of governance is the degree to which an organization is achieving its purpose. While many of the principles we will discuss have application to organizations with a wide range of purposes, our focus is narrowed to address the governing of publicly owned businesses whose purpose is to create and serve customers, the reward for which, if done well, is profitability and an accompanying increase in shareholder value.

All business organizations have multiple stakeholders whose needs must be considered to achieve sustainable success. In our current system, corporate directors are legally required to represent the best interests of the company's shareholders, not those of all of the various stakeholders. (We will discuss this further in the next chapter.) We frequently see in annual reports and press releases the mantra that "the company's goal is to increase shareholder value." It is true that shareholders generally invest in a business to make money on their investment, but the purpose of the investors should not be confused with the purpose of the business. It is in serving the needs of its stakeholders that most businesses find their purposes.

The needs of the stakeholders of a corporation might be viewed as a hierarchy, as described below.

- At the top of the hierarchy of stakeholders is the customer, whose needs must be met with goods and/or services that deliver competitive value. Ideally, businesses should treat their customers in a fashion such that a mutually beneficial and valued relationship is established and maintained. Customer satisfaction characteristically comes about because a firm's business processes are designed to consistently produce and deliver the goods and services desired by the customer. These processes include the combination of equipment and systems (technology), employees, and materials that come from suppliers.

- Consequently, the next level of the hierarchy consists of the employees who develop and operate the business processes. Given that employees in either a service or production environment are instrumental in the task of meeting customer needs, fulfilling reasonable employee expectations is crucial to a firm's success. Employees are entitled to a return on their time in the form of wages or salaries and benefits. They also want job security, acceptable working conditions, and job satisfaction.

- Similarly, the third level of stakeholders whose needs must be considered consists of suppliers, distributors, and creditors. Certainly these groups must be treated appropriately if they are to be reliable and committed. Much study has been done recently on the effective management of supply chains.

- Furthermore, the business must meet the needs of the communities in which it operates: the next level of stakeholders. A business meets these needs primarily by providing goods and/or services that the community values and jobs that the community needs. The business, however, should also be a good citizen, honoring the laws, paying appropriate taxes, preserving the environment, and participating in the governance of the community.

It follows that if a business fulfills the needs of all of the major stakeholders, the interests of the final level—ownership—will be well served. It is ideally a closed system in which the better the job the business does in meeting the needs of the other stakeholders, the more money the owners make, permitting the owners to reinvest in and share the rewards of the business, further improving their ability to meet the needs of the other stakeholders.

Shareholders are the owners of publicly owned corporations. They have delegated control to a representative board of directors, who have hired management personnel to run the business. Thus, the board of directors is ultimately responsible for representing the interests of the owners and for a business's achievement of its purpose.

The remainder of this book is dedicated to examining the role of the board of directors in the publicly owned corporation. Subsequent chapters will describe the responsibilities of a board of directors more fully, and how a board should fulfill those responsibilities to create and lead a business that achieves sustained profitability and, in the end, strives to operate in the best interests of all of its stakeholder constituencies. We will elaborate on the legal responsibilities of directors, as well as processes involved in the selection and operation of an effective, constructive board of directors.

NOTES

1. *Dartmouth College v. Woodward*, 1819.

CHAPTER 2

THE LEGAL OBLIGATIONS OF DIRECTORS

THE NEED FOR RULES

When individuals serve as directors of businesses, they assume the obligation to represent the interests of those owners who cannot represent themselves, undertaking a serious fiduciary responsibility. Effective representation, however, requires more than integrity. It also requires the competence to make sound decisions. Good directors know their limits and turn to more expert advisers when their judgment so dictates. Directors who are "ignorant but honest" fail to fulfill their obligations. Their well-intentioned incompetence can be as dangerous as dishonesty.

Even when competent individuals act with the best of intentions in the role of director, business setbacks and failures still might occur. In cases of unsatisfactory results, shareholders can scrutinize the contributing actions of the directors with the advantage of hindsight. They particularly seek answers to questions of whether the directors acted responsibly in fulfilling their obligations. At issue, though, is how "fulfilling their obligations" should be defined.

WHO MAKES THE RULES?

Governments at all levels—federal, state, and local—and various governmental agencies write, approve, and interpret the relevant laws and regulations for business enterprises. In addition, various stock exchanges and industry associations have established their own regulations and codes of conduct. As noted in the previous chapter, laws, regulations, and codes are relentlessly refined over time, typically in response to aberrant behavior in the business community.

The laws pertaining to corporations in the United States have centered on seven main goals:

- To maintain competitive markets via antitrust and fair trade laws
- To regulate noncompetitive markets, such as utilities
- To maintain a balance between capital and labor
- To ensure orderly capital markets
- To protect consumers from unsafe products and fraud
- To ensure equal access to employment, education, housing, and public accommodations
- To protect the environment

These laws and rules frame the context in which corporations must operate. There are also laws that define how corporations are to be governed. The laws that define directors' responsibilities are primarily state laws, as opposed to federal laws, because, with only a few minor exceptions, the states issue and administer corporate charters through their particular laws and regulations.

Corporate laws vary by state. The state most influential in setting corporate legal standards has been Delaware, where more than 50 percent of publicly owned, U.S. companies are incorporated.[1] Our discussion of legal standards for directors will focus on two states—Delaware and Virginia—as examples of how states approach such issues. We will note substantial similarities and differences in the codes of these two states, as they, to a large degree, define the legal spectrum across most states. All directors must recognize, however, their fundamental responsibility to understand the laws of the state in which the corporation on whose board they sit is chartered.

WHO IS RESPONSIBLE FOR GOVERNING THE AFFAIRS OF A PUBLIC CORPORATION?

The answer to the question of who is responsible for governing the affairs of a public corporation is the board of directors. The board's powers are derived from the shareholders whom they represent and are articulated in the corporation's governing documents, which include:

- The articles of incorporation
- The bylaws
- Shareholder agreements

When confronted with a corporate governance legal issue, directors should first check the corporation's governing documents, and subsequently the applicable state laws and any previously set case precedents.

State law dictates the establishment of boards of directors for most corporations. For example, the Delaware General Corporation Law Code [Paragraph 141(a)] states: "The business and affairs of every corporation organized under this chapter shall be managed by or under the direction of a board of directors, except as may be otherwise provided in this chapter or in its certificate of incorporation."

While every state has a similar statute empowering the board of directors to govern and manage the affairs of the corporation, the shareholders ultimately control the affairs of the corporation because they elect and can replace the board of directors. The shareholders normally elect directors at an annual meeting convened for that purpose and to deal with any other business that needs to be addressed. The shareholders may vote in person at the meeting or through proxies that are sent out with the notice of the meeting. The nominations for director may come from shareholders, but there is usually a slate recommended by the existing board. Most of the time, this slate runs unopposed. If there is organized opposition, there may be a contest to solicit proxies; that is, the right to vote the shares of other shareholders.

The shareholders of a corporation also have the statutory right in most states to approve major transactions or decisions, such as mergers, the sale of assets, or dissolution of the company. They may also reserve other rights in the governing documents of the corporation. In situations where the majority of stockholders of a corporation disagree with a significant action or actions of the board, the stockholders almost always win an ensuing battle, but it might take some time, particularly if the matter has to be litigated to reach a resolution.

As a matter of practice, the board of directors delegates most decisions to management, either formally or informally. Consequently, senior management typically has the authority to make day-to-day decisions in running the business. The relationship between the board and management is a crucial one, both practically, in terms of how well the business is run, and legally, in terms of who is accountable for the actions and results of the corporation. In matters of litigation, senior management always loses in a conflict with the board of directors, provided the board is truly independent of management influence.

WHAT ARE THE RESPONSIBILITIES OF DIRECTORS?

The states define the roles of directors in terms of duties. As we will note, Delaware and Virginia differ in how those duties are interpreted and articulated. In addition, in publicly owned companies, the Securities and Exchange Commission administers regulatory requirements imposed on the corporation, and hence the board, particularly with regard to insider (stock) trading and full and timely disclosure of information. The stock exchanges also have rules that prescribe certain responsibilities, enforced through the standards required for listing on the exchange.

The legal obligations of directors can be broadly summarized by the managerial duties that the law prescribes for directors. The major duties of directors are:

- The fiduciary duty
- The duty of loyalty and the duty of fair dealing
- The duty of care
- The duty not to entrench
- The duty of supervision

THE FIDUCIARY DUTY

Central to the role of a director is the fiduciary role—being trustworthy in acting in the best interests of the shareholders whom the director represents. This duty has the elements of both integrity and competence. What is the duty? It begins with an understanding of the objective of the corporation. A board of directors should have as its objective the conducting of business with a view to enhancing corporate profit and shareholder gain.[2] Courts, however, have held that even if corporate profit and shareholder gain are not enhanced, a board, in conducting its business:

(a) Must, to the same extent as a natural person, act within the boundaries set by law;

(b) May take into account ethical considerations that are reasonably regarded as appropriate to the responsible conduct of business; and

(c) May devote a reasonable amount of resources to public welfare, humanitarian, educational, and philanthropic purposes.

Directors should note that the objective to enhance "shareholder gain" is a broad term that implies everything that contributes to strengthening the economic efforts and value of the corporation. The law generally gives boards of directors the latitude to consider the long view in determining the best interests of the corporation, as well as ethics, legality, and the interests of all stakeholders in the fulfilling of their fiduciary duty.

THE DUTY OF LOYALTY AND THE DUTY OF FAIR DEALING

By assuming his or her office, the corporate director pledges to be loyal to the corporation and acknowledges that the best interests of the corporation and the shareholders must take precedence over any individual director's interest. The basic principle of this duty of loyalty is that the director should not use his or her corporate position to make a personal profit or gain other personal advantages.[3] The duty of fair dealing can be viewed as a subset of the duty of loyalty, requiring that all transactions with the corporation be handled in a forthright and open manner that is fair to the interests of the corporation.

The general rule regarding directors taking part in any business activity that is related to the business of the corporation is that a director or senior executive may not take advantage of a corporate opportunity unless the director or senior executive first offers the opportunity to the corporation, reveals a personal interest (i.e., a potential conflict of interest), and the corporation rejects the corporate opportunity. In general, a corporate opportunity is an opportunity to engage in a business activity of which a director becomes aware and believes would be of interest to the corporation. Similar to the situation of business opportunities, directors in general may not seek monetary gain by engaging in competition with the corporation. This stipulation may be altered if the corporation determines that the predicted benefits to the corporation outweigh the foreseeable harm, or if the corporation authorizes the competition after the director reveals his or her personal interest.[4]

THE DUTY OF CARE

It is incumbent on directors to act carefully in carrying out their responsibilities. This is only common sense, but it is a legal requirement, as well. The duty of care, in general, requires a director to act in the best interests of the corporation and with the care reasonably expected of "an ordinary prudent person." The director also has the duty to be informed and to make necessary inquiries to become informed. This duty, however, allows the board to delegate functions to, and rely on, others, including other directors, officers, employees, experts, and board committees. Such delegation and reliance do not eliminate the board's ultimate responsibility for oversight.[5]

What is being addressed in this duty is the reality that a director cannot know everything nor be totally expert in every facet of a business. While directors have the duty to be very careful in determining the facts, they can rely on management and experts for information they don't have and judgments about which they are not expert. This raises the question of what they should know—when they can claim ignorance as a defense. The answer, as usual, is that it depends on the situation. One of the key skills of an effective director is to understand what is relevant and to persistently seek that information, particularly when he or she has or should have a feeling of discomfort with the situation. It also emphasizes the importance of having competent and trustworthy managers and advisers, which is one more aspect of the duty of care—selecting these people well.

THE DUTY NOT TO ENTRENCH

There is some evidence that the Delaware courts are in the process of creating and imposing on directors another fiduciary duty, a "duty not to entrench." There is a body of opinion that if a corporation is not performing well, changes should be made in management. If the problem can be tracked beyond management to a board that is not fulfilling its responsibilities, changes need to be made there, as well. There are many examples of companies with poor performance where the board and management continue in place without successfully addressing the issues—in effect, they become entrenched. It emerges as an issue, for instance, when a board attempts to block a change-of-control transaction, either through the sale of the company or in a proxy fight where dissident shareholders attempt to elect a new slate of directors.

Not all opposition to a change of control, however, is evidence of entrenchment. Many times, directors think that the motives of the other party or parties attempting to force change do not represent the best interests of the shareholders as a whole, and as a result, the directors are duty bound to oppose the effort. In many cases they are correct in doing so. Fulfilling the duty not to entrench is more dependent on following good business practices in evaluating the corporate performance and the performance of management and the board than on complying with the law.

Some observers advocate term limits to avoid entrenchment. This assumes that all directors are motivated to entrench themselves, and that a board is incapable or unwilling to deal with poor performers—which is not a universally valid assumption. Further, it ignores the value of continuity and experience. While it does ensure against entrenchment, it deprives boards that are working well of effective directors at a time when recruiting talented directors is not an easy task.

THE DUTY OF SUPERVISION

The duty of supervision is a subset of the duty of care, but deals specifically with the effectiveness of the directors in exercising their oversight responsibilities. The duty of supervision addresses what directors should know about the operations of management, how they should come to know it, and what they should do when there is an issue or problem requiring attention.

As an initial step in fulfilling this duty, the board must establish policies of ethics and disclosure that set the standards of behavior for directors and senior executives. The board must also ensure that there are internal controls in place to provide accurate reporting of what is going on in the corporation. This control function is generally the responsibility of the audit committee of the board. The board must also establish policies addressing which decisions require board approval, and what information the board should regularly receive about the performance of the corporation and its various entities.

Perhaps the most important task associated with the duty of supervision is the regular meeting of the board to discuss the performance of the organization and to ask penetrating questions of management. One of the crucial skills for a director is the intuitive sense of what needs to be questioned and the willingness to be persistent in pressing for access to the relevant information. Directors must know what they need to know and insist that it be provided.

DEALING WITH HOSTILE TAKEOVER OFFERS

Dealing with hostile offers for the company is a particularly important and difficult responsibility. A hostile offer typically entails an offer to purchase the corporation made by an outside group or company without the involvement of the board of the target company. It is not uncommon for these offers to come as a surprise to the directors. Because such offers happen very infrequently, directors are often not well-informed or experienced in regard to this topic. An additional complicating factor is the tendency for hostile offers to end up in litigation as a result of their very high visibility with the shareholders.

In brief, boards may act to block hostile takeover bids for the corporation when, after having considered carefully what is in the best interests of the corporation and shareholders, they make the judgment that the takeover might jeopardize the viability of the corporation. The board may also consider the impact on groups related to the corporation other than the shareholders, so long as doing so would not significantly harm the long-term interests of the shareholders.[6]

WHAT STANDARD DETERMINES IF DIRECTORS HAVE MET THEIR RESPONSIBILITIES?

In the United States, the laws of the states and the regulations of a number of government agencies, at both the state and federal level, establish the standards of performance for directors that define their obligations. Court rulings further define these standards.

Legal challenges to decisions of a board of directors typically come from shareholders who feel that the board that has been chosen to represent their interests has somehow failed in its duties. Courts have traditionally been extremely reluctant to overturn or second-guess decisions made by a board of directors. As a result of this traditional reluctance of courts to become involved in corporate governance and decision making, the "business judgment rule" developed. Under the general business judgment rule, there is a "presumption that in making a business decision the directors of a corporation acted on an informed basis, in good faith and in the honest belief that the action was in the best interests of the company."[7] Regarding the Delaware ruling from which this rule emerged, a presumption means that the conclusion is drawn unless there is evidence to the contrary, and that the burden of proof is on the party asserting the claim, not on the board of directors defending its action.

In Virginia, the standards for the way in which directors are required to discharge their fiduciary duties are as follows:

> A director shall discharge his duties as a director, including his duties as a member of a committee, in accordance with his good faith business judgment of the best interests of the corporation.[8]

What is unusual about the Virginia law is that the Virginia courts have interpreted this section simply to require a board of directors to follow a good process in reaching its decision. If a good process is followed, the Virginia courts will not review the substance, reasonableness, or even the rationality of a board's decision.

INTERPRETATION OF THE DUTY OF CARE

As stated earlier, the duty of care requires a board of directors to act in good faith and to make informed business decisions. The consequences of breaching the duty of care are severe because the business judgment rule does not apply and the board of directors must establish the "entire fairness" of its decision. "Entire fairness" means that the shareholders have been, when all things are considered, treated fairly—that the result is fair without regard to how the decision was derived.

In order to enhance the likelihood of the proper execution of their duty of care, directors should abide by the following "commandments" or rules of guidance. Conscientious boards are likely to adhere to these in all substantial decision-making matters. The board is likely to have met its duty of care if it:

- Engages experienced legal counsel to design and manage the governance process and maintain appropriate records of the proceedings
- Does not rush important decisions; at least not unnecessarily
- Gives board members adequate prior notice of important business to be conducted at a meeting
- Distributes major documents or position papers to board members well in advance of meetings
- If possible, has one or more informational meetings, follows up with distribution of additional information in response to questions, and convenes subsequent discussion and action meetings
- Provides board members with adequate information to make an informed decision, including:
  - Access to the opinions of expert advisers
  - Management analyses and recommendations
  - Identification of and information on alternatives
  - Fairness opinions
- Does not submit to the pressures of a domineering CEO and/or others who clearly have committed to a decision prior to the board's discussions

THE DUTY OF LOYALTY IN PRACTICE

The consequences of breaching the duty of loyalty are also severe. Again, the business judgment rule does not apply, and the board of directors must establish that the challenged transaction was "fair."

As with the duty of care, there are certain commandments that establish a list of sound behaviors for conscientious boards. If these directives are followed, problems with the duty of loyalty are typically easily avoided. Duty of loyalty commandments include:

- An interested director must fully disclose any conflict of interest and the basis for it when the issue arises, and in advance of related discussions and decision.

- The interested director must not unduly influence discussion of the transaction, might need to leave the discussion, and almost certainly should abstain from voting on the issue.
- The proposed issue must be resolved by a majority of the uninvovled directors.

INDEMNIFICATION OF DIRECTORS

It is a general practice for corporations to indemnify directors against liability for their legal actions. This means that the directors are not personally liable for any damages that might result from legal acts of the board, to the extent that there are corporate assets to cover any awards to plaintiffs. Most corporations purchase directors and officers liability insurance (D&O coverage) as part of their indemnity program. Certain behaviors, such as fraud, are, by statute, excluded from indemnification.

SUMMARY

Clearly, a director individually, and a board as a whole, must act in accordance with legal standards spelled out by the state in which the business is incorporated. These laws are often complex. While no layperson can expect to fully understand them, it is essential that all directors have a working knowledge of them and know how and when to seek competent legal advice.

Of particular importance are the duties of being a director. At one level, the rules and laws are simply common sense. In particular situations, however, they can create technical compliance issues that might go well beyond common sense. Directors need not only to follow the laws but also to build records of what they have done to protect themselves from challenges that have the advantage of hindsight.

NOTES

1. Lorsch, Jay W., *Pawns or Potentate: The Reality of America's Corporate Boards* (Boston: Harvard Business School Press, 1989), p. 7.
2. The information in the section is based on paragraph 2.01 of the *Principles of Corporate Governance: Analysis and Recommendations*, assembled by the American Law Institute (St Paul, MN: American Law Institute, 1994), p. 61.

3. *Managerial Duties and Business Law* (Boston: Harvard Business School Press, 1995), p. 4.

4. This paragraph is based on Paragraphs 5.05 and 5.06 of the *Principles of Corporate Governance: Analysis and Recommendations*, assembled by the American Law Institute (St Paul, MN: American Law Institute, 1994), pp. 283-285.

5. *Ibid.*, p. 138-139.

6. *Ibid.*, p. 405.

7. *Aronson v. Lewis*, Delaware, 1984.

8. Virginia Code Section 13.1-690.

CHAPTER 3

GETTING AND KEEPING AN EFFECTIVE BOARD

INTRODUCTION

Securing the services of and retaining qualified, capable, and effective directors provides the foundation for effective corporate governance. These individuals assume the responsibility for operations, solve problems, and get the job done. The wrong people in the role of director, however, can create problems, impede progress, and even damage a firm's performance and reputation. How then should shareholders choose (elect) a specified number of qualified and respected people to represent their interests as members of a corporation's board?

In owner-managed companies, the owners may select whomever they want as directors, with the primary purpose of soliciting the best possible advice. In publicly owned companies, however, directors are not merely advisers. They are selected to represent the interests of the shareholders, and as a result, they require certain attributes beyond just bringing some competence to the board.

The process for selecting new directors and its relative formality vary greatly from company to company. In some firms, CEOs control the process, finding and presenting candidates to the board. In other situations, small groups of directors control the selection process. In either case, the process may be formal or informal. Other companies engage in a more preferable selection process, where a nominating committee of independent directors leads the board systematically through a logical and prescribed series of steps. Such a process is outlined in Exhibit 3-1.

The Board

1. Determines its target size and states it in the bylaws
2. Determines the terms of directors and obtains shareholder approval
3. Appoints a nominating committee of independent directors

The Nominating Committee

1. Determines the number of openings based on, in part, board and director performance evaluations, along with board attrition
2. Profiles the board to see what skills and experience are needed
3. Develops a pool of candidates
4. Screens the candidates, selecting the most attractive, involving the board in the process
5. Recruits the candidates
6. Nominates willing candidates and returning directors whose terms require renewal for election by the board or shareholders (as specified in the bylaws)
7. Orients new board members

EXHIBIT 3-1   The Process for Getting Effective Directors

THE SIZE OF THE BOARD

The size of a board is normally determined by the existing board and should always comply with the range or limitations established in the bylaws of the corporation. The board (or subsequent boards) may change the bylaws regarding this or any other rule, but the change must be executed in accordance with the procedures described in the bylaws themselves. Often, changes to the bylaws require approval from parties outside the board (e.g., shareholders). Choosing the size of the board is obviously an important decision.

The typical corporate board is composed of 8 to 16 directors. Larger, more mature companies tend toward the higher end of the range, while smaller, growing companies tend toward the lower end. The aim, however, is to have a breadth of expertise in order to deal effectively with the issues confronting the business. This reasoning would suggest that smaller, simpler companies would not require as many directors as larger, more complex ones. Regardless, some companies will have relatively large boards; for example, some banks have had as many as 20 to 25 directors. In these cases, the institution's desire is generally to attract to the board individuals who are important customers or influential in the community. The actual governance work in such situations is typically done by a smaller group within the board, usually an executive committee.

There are advantages and disadvantages for both smaller and larger boards. Small boards tend to be more involved and focused, and directors often find it easier to build trust and work collaboratively in a smaller group. Small boards, however, are more easily controlled by a dominant personality or clique. As boards become larger, the talent pool becomes deeper, but it is more difficult to keep a larger number of people involved and working together efficiently as a team.

THE TERMS OF DIRECTORS

Before the times of prevalent hostile (takeover) bids for companies, boards historically had been elected at the annual shareholders' meeting for a yearly term or until successors were elected. This last phrase is a technical term often included in bylaws to ensure that the board would not be reduced to an unworkable extent by the failure to elect new candidates. Under this election protocol, raiders who desired to take over businesses from current management (often with the intent of dismantling the business and selling the pieces) found that they could get an entirely new board elected with a simple majority vote, and as a result, they could control a corporation with just 51 percent of the outstanding shares.

In order to make it more difficult for anyone or any group to gain control of the board, many public corporations now employ staggered terms for directors. The board members are split into a number of classes, much like graduation classes. The classes for a given board contain approximately the same number of directors, and they typically are elected to 3- or 4-year terms. If 3-year terms were employed, it would take two years for a takeover group to gain control of the board and three years for it to install a total slate of board members. The extension of the time interval required and the higher degree of difficulty give the shareholders a better handle on the issues at stake and the motives of dissident groups.

Some shareholder activists think that all directors should stand for reelection every year to make them more responsive to the shareholders and reduce the risk of entrenched boards. While entrenched boards indeed exist, there are also raiders who will attempt to take over a business to the disadvantage of existing stakeholders. At issue, then, is which group the shareholders wish to trust to act in their best interests—their existing directors or potential raiders.

Another important topic is that of term limits for directors, which are normally subject to shareholder approval. Traditionally, boards have not employed term limits for directors. Term limits require that a director, regardless of performance, must leave the board after a stated number of years. With term limits, entrenchment is avoided, and there is an automatic means of shedding weak directors.

With term limits, though, the good directors rotate off the board with the poor ones because there is no discrimination. The loss of good directors is costly, and strong replacements are not easy to find, particularly when it is hoped they will invest heavily in a business. Also lost is the continuity of in-depth knowledge of the business. Even good, new directors take a year or more to get fully acclimated to a business. A practical solution to maintaining an effective board without term limits is to have a universal agreement among all of the directors that reelection is not automatic. The board then should employ a meaningful process to regularly evaluate the performance of the board as a collective body and of incumbent directors by their peers, taking into account the current needs of the corporation. These reviews should be annual, formal, and thorough. The results should be discussed with each director and with the entire board.

Problems with the effectiveness of the overall board can be addressed through the selection, recruitment, and election of more effective individual directors. Individual directors who are ineffective should be given the opportunity to resign from the board before the nominating committee withholds its renomination at the end of their terms.

Most boards do have mandatory retirement ages, usually somewhere between 70 and 75 years of age. This is generally regarded as a good policy. Many boards also require that a director submit his or her resignation upon a change in primary employment circumstances. The resignation may or may not be accepted by the board or nominating committee, depending on how the fellow directors perceive the change in status will influence the director's ability to function effectively.

WHO SELECTS DIRECTORS IN A PUBLIC COMPANY?

The responsibility of selecting directors may vary over time and across firms. In a startup situation, a founder or dominant personality, or a founding or controlling group, typically drives the process of selecting directors. The founder or controlling group may stay in control of the process for many years, in which case the directors selected are generally friends or business associates of the dominant person or are members of the controlling group. Startups, however, represent a small percentage of all corporations. The more common situation is for an existing board to be looking for new members as replacements of directors leaving the board or to expand the number of directors. In some cases, the founder of a business may still be active in management after a long tenure and even may be the CEO or chairman of the board. In these cases, the dominant chairman or CEO is apt to influence or control the process.

In contrast to the organization dominated by founders is the truly representative board. Such boards control the director-selection process, as opposed to the CEO or a dominant chairman, and appoint nominating committees composed of independent directors to carry out the largest part of the selection process.

The two situations described mark the limits of a continuum on which most boards fall somewhere in between. Variation derives from the strength and source of leadership.

When the CEO is in control of the nominating process, he or she may have a tendency to seek individuals who are personal acquaintances or friends and who likely will be supportive of the CEO. The result can be an apparently independent majority that, in practice, takes its cues from management and functions much like a group of insiders. Consequently, the establishment of a genuinely objective process is crucial for corporate boards.

A truly representative process would have the shareholders nominating and electing individuals to represent them. For a number of reasons, however, this process is not practical. First, many shareholders do not behave like long-term investors; indeed, they are essentially traders, who move in and out of stocks and are not particularly interested in participating in the governance of corporations in which they own stock. Institutional shareholders (including mutual funds, pension funds, and insurance or mutual companies) generally do not want to be directly represented on the boards of companies in which they invest because this would make them insiders, which, in turn, would limit their flexibility in deciding whether to buy or sell. Finally, the broad group of small, public shareholders is not a cohesive body that is organized to act together. In theory, they could identify and nominate directors, but they seldom do.

This leaves the nomination process to either the existing board, which may be inclined to perpetuate itself, or to major shareholders to nominate their representatives. When a group of shareholders becomes disenchanted with management, they may nominate a slate of directors and engage in a proxy battle. A proxy battle is an expensive process, however, and requires that the embittered shareholders either own a large block of stock or rally other shareholders to vote with them. Consequently, the nominating process for directors is usually managed by controlling shareholders and/or the current board through its nominating committee.

THE SELECTION PROCESS
FOR NEW DIRECTORS

Every board should have a nominating committee composed entirely of independent directors. This committee, also known as the *governance committee* in some situations, is responsible for the identification and selection of prospective board nominees. The task of the nominating committee is sensitive and vital—the effectiveness of a board and the quality of its decisions are linked directly to the caliber of its members.

NUMBER OF OPENINGS

Except for the unusual situations accompanying startups and mergers, openings on boards are typically created when existing directors resign, retire, or die. Openings also occur when a board decides to expand its size and occasionally in the wake of resignations or removals precipitated by the nominating committee's evaluation of director and board performance.

A growing number of companies attempt to evaluate director performance on some formal basis, but many boards still do not have a formal evaluation process. Evaluation approaches vary, ranging from the chairman of the nominating committee surveying all directors to determine if they have any problems with other directors or the way the board is functioning, to more formal written surveys undertaken and tabulated by an independent third party. In general, nominating committees do not renominate directors in cases of weak attendance, perceived conflicts of interest, failure to disclose conflicts of interest, or important changes of status. After it has determined the number of directors it will renominate, the nominating committee may calculate the number of open positions it must fill on the board.

THE BOARD PROFILE

The next step for the nominating committee is to create (or update) a profile of the types of skills and experience needed on the board. This list of desirable attributes would depend on the business or businesses in which the company engages and the strategy it expects to employ. It also would include necessary functional expertise such as accounting, finance, marketing, operations management, industry expertise, demographic expertise/diversity, along with general business experience applicable to the activities of the firm. After this step is completed, the nominating committee should compare its ideal attributes with the characteristics and experience of the returning board members and identify any gaps. The committee would then search for candidates who could complete the ideal profile of the board.

The profile of the board should address at least the following:

Independence: Inside versus Outside Directors

The board must determine the preferred distribution of inside versus outside (independent) directors. Public companies today require a clear majority of outside directors to comply with the revised listing standards of the major stock exchanges. Many companies go beyond this requirement and limit the inside directors to the CEO. Some companies may have one or two additional inside directors who make a special contribution to the board. For example, a president or chief operating officer who is being groomed for CEO succession might be invited to join the board to ensure a smooth transition when the current CEO retires.

Retired CEOs and Other Retired Executives

Retired CEOs and other executives of the company normally do not remain on the board beyond a one-year transition period after their retirement. Under current laws, they would not be considered independent until at least three years have elapsed from the end of their employment. The advantages of retaining former CEOs include access to their knowledge of the business and the strong likelihood of their having a major stake in it. The disadvantage of their retention is the lack of independence arising from their ties to management.

Moreover, a former CEO might create problems for the new CEO, particularly if the new CEO wants to make major changes. It would be difficult for a retired CEO to openly oppose the recommendations or actions of the new CEO without creating unfortunate tension for the other directors. In situations where the retiring CEO is a major shareholder and has a long record of success and good personal chemistry with the new CEO, a board might lean toward making an exception, but even under these circumstances, retaining a retiring CEO is a risky practice.

Major Shareholders

Individuals who own large blocks of stock often want to be on the board or have a representative on the board. This is acceptable if the individual recognizes that every director must represent all shareholders. It is not appropriate for an individual to represent solely his or her own interests. Nominating committee members should be aware that shareholders owning a substantial portion of any class of the company's stock might not be considered independent for some purposes.

The Company's Lawyers, Consultants, Customers, and Suppliers

In the past, it was not uncommon for a firm's primary lawyer or banker to be on the board, or for other directors to draw fees for providing consulting or other services to the company. There is a growing recognition that this behavior represents a conflict of interest and should be avoided. Many, if not most, public companies now prohibit directors from receiving any compensation beyond director's fees.

Expertise

A company needs a board of competent individuals who are diverse in talent and strong in character. As noted previously, well-meaning incompetence is not acceptable today. A typical board should include individuals with a mix of expertise in the business of the company, in running companies of similar size, and in activities in which the company is active, such as strategic planning, mergers and acquisitions, technology development, or R&D. A company should also want its board to include individuals with functional competence, particularly in accounting and internal controls, financial management, marketing, production/operations, and compensation or human relations. In fact, new governance regulations require that a subset of directors on each board of publicly traded companies demonstrate financial literacy or expertise. Typically, a candidate for the board should have multiple characteristics desired for board service.

THE SEARCH AND SELECTION PROCESS

After the nominating committee has identified the needs and desires of the board regarding new members, its next step is to begin looking for appropriate candidates. A few companies use professional search firms for this task, but most will ask current board members to put forward the names of potential candidates. The board also may seek suggestions from other groups or individuals familiar with the firm, such as investment bankers, lawyers, and customers. After an initial list of candidates has been compiled, the nominating committee should perform a preliminary screening. This typically involves collecting reported information about the candidates and their credentials.

The last step in this private phase of identifying candidates for board service is to arrive at a priority ordering of the potential candidates. This ordering may be done across the entire list or in categories representing the skills or experience needed for the board. The nominating committee then should analyze the entire list in order to decide those candidates who best fit the needs of the board and company going forward. This step, like all the steps that precede it, should be a board-confidential activity. When the board moves on to researching and recruiting new members, this privacy will no longer be required.

DUE DILIGENCE AND RECRUITMENT

The next step for the nominating committee is to conduct its due diligence, meaning really getting to know the individual candidates and their reputations. After determining that the preferred individuals might be interested in joining the board, several members of the committee, perhaps joined by other members of the board or the CEO, should meet with the candidates individually. References should also be checked thoroughly, and the committee should assess whether there would be good chemistry between the candidate and the other board members. Finally, it is essential that the individual demonstrate an interest and desire to be on the board and that he or she not have prior commitments that would conflict with this service. The due diligence process becomes recruitment when the committee has decided that it wants the individual. In fact, due diligence and recruitment may proceed virtually simultaneously.

The actual recruitment of prospective nominees can take a variety of approaches, but the most common is recruitment through personal relationships with one or more existing board members. It may involve visits to the company facilities, meetings with key managers, and social occasions with current directors. At such gatherings, the board is usually attempting to impress the candidate with the attractiveness of the opportunity to serve on the board and the effectiveness of the board and management. Board members also should emphasize the contribution the recruit might make to the board and the company.

The committee should keep in mind that these interviews and meetings serve two purposes. The first is for the members of the board and the candidates to come to know each other better, particularly in order to determine if there is a fit between the candidates and the needs of the organization and the culture of the board. The second is to recruit the candidates—to sell them on becoming members of the board. The committee should aim to be in the position of having the candidates willing to join the board if invited, yet not being obligated to extend the invitation.

The process of due diligence and recruitment should answer some essential questions, including the following:

Is the candidate willing and able to make a meaningful commitment to the job of being a director of this company?

The best directors are conscientious by nature and have the ability to control some or all of their own time. They also have or are willing and able to make a substantial (for them) investment in the business. Stock ownership is an important method of aligning the interests of the director with that of the other shareholders. An additional consideration for directors is the location of the company headquarters relative to where they live and work. Travel time to and from committee and board meetings can be substantial and should be considered in assessing a candidate's ability to serve.

Does the candidate have unquestioned character and integrity?

Because shareholders entrust directors with complete authority to act on their behalf, the shareholders must be confident that the directors are of the highest character and adhere to sound ethical standards. All candidates for director must have a history of straightforward, honest business dealings.

Can the candidate function effectively in a group?

A board functions as a collective body. The group must be able to have open, candid discussions and handle disagreements as it seeks answers, if not consensus. If there is always total agreement among the board members, problems exist either in the board's functioning or its composition. It is the exploration and discussion of differing viewpoints that enables a board to find the best decisions. Individuals who do not know how to collaborate effectively in complex situations will not contribute to the board's highest functioning. Thus, regardless of their other attributes, board members must be capable of functioning effectively on a team and engaging in no-fault confrontation. They must also be willing to express contrary views in the face of opposition.

MUTUAL AGREEMENT

In completing its duties, the nominating committee must make a decision whether to recommend an individual for membership on the board. If the committee decides in favor of recommendation, it must then obtain the board's agreement. What follows is typically a three-step process, but the procedures may move so quickly that the steps appear to be almost simultaneous.

The board first must indicate its willingness to elect or nominate an individual. The board then offers the individual the post or nomination, and after receiving an acknowledgment of willingness to serve, the board elects the individual or agrees to recommend the individual to the shareholders, who then vote on the election. On occasion, the nominating committee must first address reservations and concerns a candidate might have regarding board service. It is unusual, though, for the process to fail at this point. A lack of interest or willingness to serve normally becomes apparent earlier in the process.

THE NOMINEE'S DECISION TO SERVE

After being approached by a current board member, a candidate for board service should perform some research before agreeing to stand for election. It is incumbent on the prospective nominee to determine precisely what a director's full responsibilities are and to judge his or her individual ability to fulfill them. It is also the task of the prospective nominee to be certain that no real or perceived conflicts of interest exist. Finally, a nominee should be comfortable linking his or her reputation to that of the company and the board. Due diligence is an important process for the nominee as well as the company.

It is reasonable for a company to ask why a nominee might be interested in joining a board, as the motive often affects commitment. The primary reasons tend to be the opportunity to gain additional experience, to network, and to contribute. Prestige and remuneration can play a role, although many good directors need neither due to past accomplishments. For some, it might be camaraderie or friendship, but this leads to less independence.

There is also a growing group of successful executives who are retired yet welcome an opportunity to stay active and challenged. They represent a pool of proven talent, often have extensive personal networks, and can make excellent directors.

THE ELECTION OF DIRECTORS

The election of directors traditionally takes place at the annual meeting of shareholders. The shareholders elect directors who will be legally charged with representing their interests. In the case of interim vacancies, the bylaws generally permit the board to fill the vacancies for the balance of the unexpired terms or until the next annual meeting. The number of nominees proposed by the nominating committee is normally identical to the number of vacant seats.

Most companies also permit the shareholders to nominate candidates for the board. Such candidates may be placed on the proxy mailed to shareholders in advance of the shareholders meeting and returned to the company for voting. It seldom happens that a write-in candidate (or candidates) receives a substantial number of votes except during a battle for control of the company between shareholder factions. The resulting dispute is known as a "proxy contest," as mentioned earlier.

Directors are usually elected to terms of one to three years. Terms begin and expire on the date of the annual meeting of shareholders. Removal of a serving director is nearly impossible, lacking some cause that could lead to his or her resignation. This rigidity in the matter of board service puts a high premium on a thorough process of identification, recruitment, and election of directors.

MAINTAINING BOARD EFFECTIVENESS

It takes some time—often a year or more—for a board member to become adequately familiar with the financial and operational performance of a business to become an effective director. The process of familiarization, though, can be accelerated with an orientation process. Director orientation should require that new directors read the company's articles of incorporation, bylaws, and employee handbook. It should also include visits to plants and customers and meetings with officers, top executives, and other key managers. A useful addition to director orientation is a session on legislative awareness, which should address laws and regulations relevant to proper execution of the responsibilities of director.

Considering the very long time frame over which corporations function, we recognize the value of the investment in a director orientation program. Many businesses continue on for decades, requiring an orderly series of transitions in both boards and CEOs. It is therefore important to take a long-term view in the process of board selection and education. Boards do not suddenly become exceptional or troubled. The movement of boards to excellence or mediocrity takes place gradually over an extended period of time, hardly overnight. As terms expire, the relative effectiveness of an entire board is shaped by each sequential selection decision.

SUMMARY

Strong boards evolve from a culture that includes a strong, independent set of directors and a well-functioning nominating committee charged with identifying, recruiting, and obtaining the election of people meeting the criteria described earlier. Weak boards, on the other hand, almost invariably emanate from a dominant CEO who is able to control the nominating process to the extent that his or her cronies come to dominate the board. The CEO then has total control, and the board no longer represents the best interests of the shareholders in the sense intended. Thus the selection process by which the board is formed must ensure that each appointment of a new director moves the total board further in the direction of excellence with regard to board effectiveness. A failure to do so could put the quality of the board on a self-perpetuating path toward mediocrity or even demise.

With a competent board in place, board leadership must organize the work of the board so that it can be efficient and effective. The next chapter addresses how this can be accomplished.

CHAPTER 4

HOW AN EFFECTIVE BOARD ORGANIZES ITS WORK

After a corporation is formed and a board is in place, the board must organize itself to fulfill its responsibilities. This chapter describes how a board of directors is generally organized to oversee the management of the corporation.

THE BYLAWS

An important first task of a newly formed corporation is to write the bylaws, which set out the rules under which the board will operate. The company's lawyer usually drafts the bylaws. Essentially, the bylaws should establish in writing how the directors want to function but also, in anticipation of disputes that might occur, articulate rules that ensure an orderly process of majority rule.

When conflict or disagreement arises among the directors or involving the shareholders, the bylaws can become very important in finding resolution. An illustration of the importance of bylaws—and directors' understanding of them—follows.

In an actual situation where there was a bitter disagreement on whether the chairman/CEO should continue in his role, the 12 directors on the firm's board were evenly divided on the issue. While the directors were negotiating a resolution, one of the directors opposed to the chairman was disabled by a stroke. The bylaws stated that the chairman could call an official meeting without stating the subject to be discussed as long as a quorum, defined as a majority of the directors, in this case seven, was present. This meant that the six favoring the reelection of the chairman plus at least one in opposition would have to be present to take a vote.

The chairman chose to call a meeting, per the bylaws. Prior to the meeting, a relative of the ill director used a power of attorney to submit the director's resignation from the board, creating an opening. The opposing side did not know of this scheme until the meeting began, at which time the resignation was submitted and accepted.

The chairman's supporters then immediately elected a replacement director who was friendly to the chairman on a vote of six to five. The individual who was elected then joined the meeting, creating a seven-to-five majority. Concerned about quorum issues at future meetings, the new majority changed the bylaws to add two more directors, bringing the total to 14 and the quorum requirement to 8. On passing the amendment, the majority immediately elected two additional directors and attained a working majority of nine who favored the chairman versus the five who did not.

If the opposing side had not been caught by surprise and had understood the bylaws, its members could have disrupted the process simply by leaving the meeting and destroying the quorum. They did not think to use the bylaws strategically to their own advantage, and their lack of recognition of this possibility played out in their defeat.

The bylaws usually address the following:

- The rules by which persons standing for election are voted on by the shareholders.
- How persons standing for election will be selected.
- The number of directors who will sit on the board.
- The number of "insiders" and "outsiders."
- The length of the terms of directors.
- The conditions under which directors may be removed from office, including any limitations such as age, attendance, the requirement that directors submit a resignation letter when they change their employment status, and "for cause." The bylaws spell out the definitions of "for cause."
- The board and corporate officer titles and duties, and the procedures for electing them.
- The level of compensation for directors.
- The board committees and their charges.
- Details about the annual meeting of shareholders.
- Details about special meetings of the shareholders, and who can call them for what reasons.
- The conditions under which voting proxies will be issued to the shareholders.
- Authority to call a board meeting, and the notice required.

- Frequency of board meetings.
- How the agenda will be prepared and by whom.
- Definition of a quorum.

THE ANNUAL MEETING OF THE SHAREHOLDERS

The bylaws of a corporation should specify when its annual meeting will be held as well as the rules by which it will be run. It would appear, initially, that shareholders should have fairly broad rights in calling meetings to discuss and vote on the affairs of the business. In reality, though, businesses have been compelled to institute constraints due to historical abuses of vocal minorities who pushed agendas not shared by the majority of the shareholders. As noted previously, such agendas might focus on political or social issues, or they might involve intentions on the part of a few individuals to gain control of a majority of the shares of the corporation at a low value in order to pursue their own interests.

The shareholders' annual meeting is a major event for a public corporation. These meetings are scheduled routinely at a convenient time after the close of business at the end of the corporation's fiscal year and following the availability of audited financial statements, typically 90 to 120 days after the end of a company's fiscal year. The board provides the shareholders with an annual report of the results and condition of the company, as well as its outlook for the future. This report is usually delivered in writing prior to the annual meeting.

A proxy statement is normally issued with the annual report in advance of the annual meeting. The proxy statement discloses the business to be discussed at the annual meeting and solicits proxy votes to be sent in by those who do not plan to attend and vote in person. These "proxies" appoint selected directors or officers to vote the proxy as directed by the shareholder. In practice, all shareholders are encouraged to send in their proxies in advance even if they plan to attend the meeting.

Annual meetings can vary from very short, legal formalities to very large, extravagant affairs that promote the company as a good investment. They normally deal with the election of directors and the approval of the independent auditing firm. The shareholders also vote on other matters requiring approval, such as executive compensation plans, including stock option plans, the authorization of the sale of new stock, or the adoption of a poison pill plan to defend against hostile takeover attempts.

Special shareholder meetings are conducted similarly to an annual meeting, except that they are called for a specific, special purpose. Perhaps the most frequent purpose is to vote on some major merger or acquisition.

DEFENSIVE MEASURES

There are numerous measures available to board members to assist them in retaining control of a corporation. Three of the most prominent measures are described below.

THE "POISON PILL"

Poison pill is the name given to a defensive measure addressing hostile takeovers. It is not intended to deter hostile takeovers, but rather to force any potential buyers of a corporation to negotiate with the board rather than appealing directly to the shareholders. Critics argue that a pill makes it more difficult to dislodge the entrenched management of underperforming companies, which is true. Without effective defensive measures, however, it is easier for corporate raiders to attempt to acquire companies at lower than fair prices. Shareholders have to decide which group is better intentioned regarding their interests, which in practice can only be answered case by case.

A poison pill functions by establishing a rights offering to existing shareholders that is triggered by a raider's obtaining a predetermined percentage of the ownership of the company, generally in the range of 15 to 20 percent of the outstanding shares. If a raider attempts to cross that threshold level of ownership without the board's approval, the share offering is automatically triggered, which requires the board to issue existing shareholders the right to purchase additional shares at a very low price, say pennies per share. The new shares issued to preexisting shareholders would result in the dilution of the raider's ownership to the point that it is virtually worthless.

Poison pills of this type are so effective that one has never been triggered, strongly suggesting that they do deter raiders. Furthermore, studies indicate that companies with shareholder rights plans in place obtain a higher price for a sales transaction (in the event of a sale of the company) than those without one, an obvious influence being the mere existence of the poison pill threat.

STAGGERED TERMS

Another defensive measure available to boards is the use of staggered terms for directors. As described in the previous chapter, in a staggered-term plan, directors are elected for multiple-year terms, with three-year terms appearing to be the most popular. The directors are divided into classes, with one class coming up for reappointment each year. Thus, if there are three classes of directors, then three-year terms are employed. When staggered terms are initially adopted, one class is elected for one year, one for two years, and one for three years. Thereafter, each class is elected for a three-year term.

When staggered terms are in place, a raider cannot take over the board immediately—and hence the company—by changing out the majority of the board in one year. The raider would require at least two years to gain control of the board.

ABILITY TO CHANGE THE BYLAWS

Because all circumstances cannot be anticipated at the time the bylaws are written, a mechanism to address the inevitable need for change must be included. Typically, a majority vote of the board is required to change the bylaws, except for those provisions that require shareholder approval. Certain changes may require a supermajority (e.g., 60 percent, two-thirds, or 80 percent) of the board or the shareholders in favor. With the ability to change the bylaws, the board has the option to craft additional defensive measures as the need arises.

THE ELECTION OF CORPORATE OFFICERS

The previous chapter discussed the general process of nominating and electing directors. Here we will examine the requirements for and election of officers of the board. State statutes generally require that a company's officers include a president and a secretary, with requirements for other officers spelled out in the bylaws. The identification or election of corporate officers has important legal implications in that officers are deemed to have the authority to bind the corporation. Because they are designated as legitimate agents of the corporation, their actions are assumed to be those of the corporation. In addition, officers and directors are usually indemnified for their actions unless there is misconduct of some sort, and frequently insurance is purchased in support of the indemnity. A brief discussion of the roles of certain corporate officers follows.

CHAIRMAN OR LEAD DIRECTOR

The major governance decision with regard to officers is whether to have a CEO who is also the chairman of the board or to separate the two positions. Approximately 85 percent of publicly held corporations in the United States combine the chairman of the board and the CEO positions in one job, while this combination is virtually unheard of in Europe.

An interesting question arises when the CEO and chairman positions are held by the same executive: Who manages the process of overseeing the performance of the CEO? For the CEO/chairman to do so is clearly a conflict of interest. With a desire for more oversight and less risk of scandal, boards are increasingly following the growing trend toward separating the two jobs and electing a nonemployee chairman. The CEO normally holds the title of president in these cases.

OTHER OFFICERS

A related issue is whether to have executive officers, in addition to the CEO, on the board as inside directors. When there are insiders on the board, the outside directors come to know management better and get a broader exposure to the workings of the company. One danger to this arrangement, however, is that the managers who are subordinate to the CEO normally will have great difficulty disagreeing with their superior. If this is not the case, the alternative danger is that the inside directors could undercut the leadership of the CEO. Regardless, it is mandatory that all public boards have more outside directors than inside directors.

The hierarchy of officer titles within a firm varies widely. Exhibit 4-1 illustrates three typical schemes. The lower titles, vice president, controller, treasurer, and secretary, may all be accompanied by assistant titles as well. It should be noted that there is a distinction between corporate officer titles and titles that do not designate corporate officers. In most organizations, there is a range of titles such as manager or

Complex Organization	Simple Organization	Small Organization
Chairman/CEO	Chairman/CEO	President/CEO
Vice Chairmen	President/Chief Operating Officer	Executive Vice President /Chief Operating Officer
President/Chief Operating Officer	Senior Vice Presidents	Vice Presidents
Executive Vice Presidents	Vice Presidents	Secretary/Treasurer
Senior Vice Presidents	Treasurer	
Vice Presidents	Secretary	
Controller		
Treasurer		
Secretary		

EXHIBIT 4-1   Typical Hierarchies of Officer Titles

director that are not corporate titles. The precise designation varies from firm to firm

The organization scheme chosen by a corporation depends on the nature of the business and the philosophy of the management. Many large companies operate with the belief that the prestige of a title enhances a person's effectiveness, both inside and outside the organization, and that it serves as a morale booster for individual managers.

On the other hand, some management teams advocate a much flatter organizational structure with less emphasis on rank. They want as little distinction between levels as possible, placing more emphasis on performance and teamwork. These organizations do not think leaders need titles to be effective.

THE BOARD COMMITTEES

A board of directors normally does its work through a well-organized committee structure that partitions the work of the board. There are several benefits to this approach. It allows a few directors to concentrate on specific issues in much more detail than the entire board could manage, and it also takes advantage of the individual expertise of the directors. The committee structure thus provides for the efficient use of time and expertise.

Committee work can be done in one of two ways. The board can delegate certain decisions to the relevant committees, or it can ask the committees to study the issues and report back to the board with recommendations. Each committee should have a clear charge stating its responsibilities, which are usually contained in its charter. Each committee should also record minutes of its meetings and regularly report its findings and actions to the full board.

Most boards have the following standing committees in some form:

- Executive committee
- Committee of outside directors
- Compensation committee
- Audit committee
- Nominating or governance committee

Boards may have other standing committees that reflect their particular circumstances. They may also appoint ad hoc or special committees, which generally are used for very specific, important, and temporary tasks such as studying merger opportunities or investigating a specific managerial issue. Each of the standing committees is described briefly below, following a short discussion of principles applying to all committees of a board.

GUIDING PRINCIPLES FOR COMMITTEES

Each committee of a board should:

- Have members who are intellectually independent, qualified, and diligent
- Have a written charter approved by the board that describes its mission, organization, roles and responsibilities, and policies and practices
- Be properly informed by and have open and candid communications with management
- Meet regularly and deal promptly and decisively with issues, keeping the full board informed about its discussions and actions

THE EXECUTIVE COMMITTEE

The executive committee can be used in at least the following three ways:

- It may provide a backup mechanism that acts for the board when time or circumstances make it difficult to bring a quorum of the full board together. Members are chosen, among other criteria, for their ability to be available on short notice. When the executive committee acts in this capacity, it should notify other members of the board in advance, if possible, to get their views, and should present a full report on its actions to the board at the next meeting.
- It may be composed of the chairs of the other standing committees, and it may be the means for coordinating their activities.
- It may be a senior board to which all issues are presented before going to the whole board. This is usually found when there is a very large board that does not meet as frequently as the situation requires. One disadvantage of this arrangement is that it may create an "in group" and an "out group," in appearance, if not in fact.

THE COMMITTEE OF OUTSIDE DIRECTORS

This committee is composed of the outside, or independent, directors. The chairperson of this committee is elected by the other independent directors and commonly serves as the lead director if the CEO also serves as chairman. If the board has a nonemployee chairman, he or she typically chairs this committee.

The committee of outside directors normally meets at the end of each board meeting without the CEO or any other inside members of the board to discuss any issues that it deems appropriate. These issues usually involve the CEO's performance or disagreements among the directors with the CEO's positions or the company's operating results. The purpose of the discussions is to explore and articulate an independent review. The lead director follows up, acting as the intermediary with the CEO unless the committee asks that the CEO return to the meeting to discuss an issue. The company's general counsel often advises this committee, particularly when the committee must address issues that have legal implications.

THE COMPENSATION COMMITTEE

The compensation committee should be composed of independent directors. It is charged with designing and administering compensation and benefit plans of the key executives and usually also addresses performance appraisals.

Because fringe benefits are normally part of the compensation package, the management of retirement plans frequently falls under this committee. Retirement plans, however, often have a large quantity of assets, requiring effective investment management. As a result, the responsibility of managing retirement benefits can be delegated to a subcommittee or separate standing committee of the board.

Staff assistance for the compensation committee is normally provided by the senior human resources officer, and frequently the committee employs outside compensation consultants, particularly to design plans intended to establish external parity. ·

THE AUDIT COMMITTEE

In today's climate, the audit committee has assumed even greater importance than in the past. The primary purpose of the audit committee is overseeing the accounting and financial reporting processes of the company and audits of the financial statements. The audit committee should:

- Encourage a strong operating culture that espouses basic values of integrity, legal compliance, forthright financial reporting, and strong financial controls.
- Have direct, independent communications with both the external and the internal auditors.
- Make it unequivocally clear that the ultimate accountability of both internal and external auditors is to the audit committee and the full board.
- Guarantee compliance with generally accepted accounting principles (GAAP) and ensure full, accurate, and timely disclosure of all relevant information to the public.

In the past, the audit committee's emphasis in most companies was on accurate financial reporting. Over the years, the audit committee's function has expanded into oversight of financial controls, often using an internal audit staff. More recently, these responsibilities have tended to expand to overseeing the processes that monitor compliance with laws, regulations, and the corporate code of conduct, and to conducting special investigations.

Internal control is a process implemented by the board of directors, management, and other personnel, designed to provide reasonable assurance regarding the achievement of objectives in the following three areas:

- Effectiveness and efficiency of operations
- Reliability of financial reporting
- Compliance with laws and regulations.

It should be noted that internal control goes beyond the financial function of the business to include the much broader areas of operations and legal compliance. The internal control function should include managing the control environment, risk assessment, control activities, information and communications, and the monitoring efforts.

Given their crucial role in overseeing the processes related to the reporting and auditing of financial results, audit committees are dependent on members' abilities to ask the tough questions and pursue any line of inquiry until they fully understand and are satisfied with the answers. Audit committee members must be good judges of the character of the managers with whom they deal, and they must create a culture that minimizes the risk of strong or deceitful personalities cutting corners or not providing full disclosure.

THE NOMINATING OR GOVERNANCE COMMITTEE

As noted in the previous chapter, the nominating committee, sometimes known as the governance committee, identifies and recruits new members of the board when openings occur. In many companies, this committee has also begun to manage the process of evaluating the performance of the board as a whole as well as that of individual members. Based on these evaluations, directors are or are not renominated for a new term. The evaluation results should also be used to find ideas for ever-improving the board's interactions and performance. Exhibit 4-2 presents a sample questionnaire for the annual self-evaluation of a board.

This committee also may be responsible for administering directors' compensation, and if it also serves as the governance committee, for overseeing the governance process and practices, and maintaining and ensuring compliance with the bylaws.

Questions are answered as Acceptable or Needs Improvement. There is a place for comments following each question.

Structure and Effectiveness of Board and Committee Meetings

1. Timing and length of board meetings
2. Timing and length of committee meetings
3. Board's input and review of meeting agendas
4. Use of time and coverage of subjects at meetings
5. Director participation in board and committee meetings
6. Timely resolution of important issues
7. Candid and constructive executive sessions
8. Structure and membership of committees
9. Effectiveness and reports of committees

Board Membership

10. Appropriate skills, experience, and diversity reflected in the board's membership
11. Qualifications to meet governance needs of the company reflected in board membership
12. Process for identification, consideration, recruitment, and nomination of prospective new directors
13. Orientation program for new directors

Board Materials and Communications

14. Quality, adequacy, and timeliness of materials provided for review in advance of meetings
15. Quality and adequacy of management presentations and other material regarding
    - Strategic evaluation and planning
    - Financial situation and results
    - Personnel and compensation matters
    - Compliance and ethics programs
    - Legal and policy issues
16. Access to senior management inside and outside of board meetings for relevant information
17. Communications with external and internal advisers such as auditors, legal counsel, investment and compensation and benefits specialists as appropriate

EXHIBIT 4-2   Sample Annual Board Self-Evaluation Questionnaire

Other Board Duties and Responsibilities

18. Board attention to strategic issues
19. Board discussion and directions of the company's strategic goals and challenges
20. Board review of budgets and plans
21. Board monitoring of effectiveness of board committees and management generally
22. Board monitoring of performance and results compared to budgets and plans
23. Communications with CEO on goals, expectations, and concerns
24. Effective and timely performance evaluation by board of the CEO and other senior management
25. Board attention to management development and succession planning for CEO and other senior management
26. Effectiveness of internal controls and risk management and of systems for monitoring compliance with applicable laws, regulations, and policies
27. Director disclosure of actual or potential conflicts of interest
28. Overall effectiveness of board in meeting its governance responsibilities

EXHIBIT 4-2   (*Continued*)

THE BOARD MEETING

The Board meeting is the centerpiece of a board's activities. It is difficult to characterize a typical board meeting; they vary with the company's circumstances and the personalities of the directors. They can be very short and informal or just the opposite, lengthy and ceremonial. Board meetings can be friendly and relaxed or adversarial and tense, efficient and no nonsense or rambling with a great deal of irrelevant discussion. Probably the single most influential variable contributing to the tone of a meeting is the style or personality of the leader or leaders. When there is a dominating leader or clique present among the board, decisions may be made beforehand, and the board's actions become mere formalities with a minimum of discussion. At the other end of the spectrum is the truly deliberative body, in which the directors individually and as a group take their responsibilities seriously. Here the leadership is less concerned about control and more concerned about a rule of reason. The leader wants orderly processes that tap into the diverse abilities of the directors and make it comfortable for each member to participate in and contribute to the discussions. This type of board meeting is described in this chapter.

A number of factors make achieving board effectiveness a challenge. Three factors that are primary among these are described below:

- Time limitations

    Boards spend relatively few hours together, and usually have a great deal to cover. Consequently, board members must make wise choices about what needs their attention and how much time they can and should devote to a topic.

- Asymmetry of information

    The CEO and management are employed full time to tend to the affairs of the business and as a result have a deep understanding of the company's situation. It is a challenge, though, for directors to obtain a thorough enough understanding to have meaningful discussions with management. Effective communication of the details requires that management efficiently present accurate and complete summaries of the situation without slanting the information to reflect their own personal views. Directors should be skilled at active listening as well as analyzing and probing arguments.

- Perspective

    There is a great tendency to spend time on the niceties of form as opposed to the substance of issues, with an overemphasis on what has happened in the past. Clearly, understanding where the company is and how it got there is important. But strong boards are future-oriented. Focusing on the future is, of course, much more difficult work for the board, but it is precisely here that its intrinsic value to shareholders resides.

PREPARATION FOR A MEETING

An effective board meeting begins with careful preparation. A prerequisite for a productive meeting is to have good staff work carried out in advance that provides relevant information, frames issues, explains alternatives, and preferably offers reasoned recommendations that are supported by analyses. Ideally, the material should be distributed to the board sufficiently in advance so that members may study it carefully, become comfortable with the topics to be considered, and arrive at the board meeting prepared with questions or informed positions on the topics of discussion.

Another major element of preparation is committee work. Unless the board is very small, it generally does the bulk of its work in committees. The committees meet prior to the board meeting and cover topics for which they are responsible in much more detail than is possible at the board meeting. They must have access to key managers in their areas of responsibility, as well as to outside experts when needed.

Committees report their findings, recommendations, and actions to the full board. They should be able to bring their recommendations to the board with sufficient logic and supporting documentation to have wide credibility with the other board members. While the full board does not want to redo committee work, the other directors are free, and, in fact, obligated, to question the committees' recommendations and vote their own views.

THE MECHANICS OF MEETINGS

The meetings of effective boards have a tone of teamwork and collaboration. Professional colleagues come together to focus on a common interest, which is the welfare of the organization. They know and trust each other. Each understands his or her role. While they have their own opinions, they listen well to what others have to say and integrate those ideas into their own thinking. In search of the best answers, they work hard to find consensus but remain comfortable with the inevitability of disagreement.

In addition to directors, there is frequently a corporate secretary in attendance who takes the minutes of the meeting. Most companies will bring in key managers from time to time to make presentations on operations or proposals. Some boards, on the other hand, will have key members of management and the general counsel attend the entire meeting, except for executive sessions, to answer questions and observe proceedings. This practice, however, is not recommended as it can inhibit candid discussion, particularly in times of controversy. It is a common practice in many boards that people who attend for special reasons leave after their business with the board is concluded.

The chairman of the board runs the board meeting and prepares the agenda in collaboration with the CEO if the positions are not combined. While aiming to provide attendees a chance to speak as they wish, the chairman must strive to keep the discussion on point and within time constraints. Exhibit 4-3 shows topics the agenda often includes for a regular meeting.

The corporation's secretary should prepare careful minutes of the proceedings of each meeting. The minutes do not have to be in great detail, though, and they should not attempt to report verbatim the discussions, as a court transcript records testimony. Rather, they should identify the topics covered during the meeting, summarize any major points discussed, and record actions taken. Because they can be used in legal actions, it is prudent to have the minutes reviewed by an attorney. Directors should read the minutes carefully, with the understanding that once they are approved, they become the official record of the deliberations and actions of the board.

Effective boards manage their affairs through efficient use of their committees and well-run board meetings. At the heart of their success, though, is the relationship between the board and the CEO. We will address many facets of this important association in the next chapter.

Item	Discussion
Quorum	There must be a quorum as defined in the bylaws to have an official meeting.
Approval of the agenda	Some boards will give the directors an opportunity to modify the agenda.
Approval of the minutes of prior meetings	Most bylaws require the approval of minutes before they are official. These are generally mailed out in advance, preferably reasonably close to the completion of the prior meeting.
Consent items	Some boards will address routine action items that require no discussion at this point. Examples might be the approval of minutes, declaration of a regular dividend, and annual meeting notices. Related material should be mailed in advance of the meeting so that no briefing is required. Directors can, of course, ask for discussion, but in general, this is an efficient way of disposing of routine administrative business.
Committee reports and actions	Typically, the chair of each committee will report to the board on the outcome of committee meetings, including major issues discussed, actions taken, and recommendations for board action. These recommendations are normally discussed and acted on at this time.
Current operations reports	The CEO reports on the results of the last period and near-term prospects. The CFO may give a financial report, and the CEOs or presidents of major divisions or subsidiaries may also report.
Briefings or proposals	At this point, management may brief the board on topics or issues of interest or bring proposals to the board for action. Major capital investment decisions are presented at this time. In the case of a major proposal, such as the acquisition of another company, the entire board meeting might be devoted to the single topic.

EXHIBIT 4-3   Sample Board Meeting Agenda

Item	Discussion
Executive session	Many boards go into a routine executive session at the end of each meeting. (They may also go into executive session at other times in the course of the meeting.) Management and the CEO are asked to leave, and the directors are given an opportunity to discuss privately issues of interest or concern. The chairman or lead director may be instructed to take messages to the CEO, or the CEO may be asked to return to the room to participate in the discussion. For boards with a committee of outside directors, this session is considered a meeting of that committee.
Adjournment	The meeting ends with a vote to adjourn, or in less formal situations, a declaration by the chairman that the meeting is adjourned.

EXHIBIT 4-3   (*Continued*)

CHAPTER 5

THE BOARD-CEO RELATIONSHIP

INTRODUCTION

Among the most important responsibilities of a board of directors is the selection of the chief executive officer (CEO). This duty has a profound impact on the success of a corporation and is the exclusive responsibility of the board. The results for the company and the shareholders can be exceptional when the board makes a good choice. A poor choice, on the other hand, can produce an expensive disaster. Furthermore, even a mediocre choice can lead to a large cost of unrealized opportunities. The strength and effectiveness of a leader can and should have a marked impact on the operating results of a business.

CEO SUCCESSION AND SELECTION

Except in startup situations, a board faced with hiring a CEO always faces the task of selecting a successor to an existing CEO. The circumstances under which the board must make this selection vary tremendously, with major variables encompassing the following:

- Reasons for the change in leadership
- The time interval during which the board has notice of the impending change
- The current condition of the business and the trend or trajectory of its results

Exhibit 5-1 shows various permutations of these important variables involved in the replacement of a CEO.

Reasons for Change	Notice Timing	Business Situation Condition	Business Situation Trajectory
1. Normal retirement 2. Death or disability 3. Resignation 4. Termination	1. Long-term anticipation 2. Short-term anticipation 3. Unexpected	1. Strong 2. Stable 3. Weak 4. Crisis	1. Positive; improving results 2. Stable; constant results 3. Negative; declining results

EXHIBIT 5-1   Important Variables Involved in the Replacement of a CEO

In the section that follows, we will examine three possible scenarios derived from certain common combinations of the variables. The scenarios are:

- Scenario 1: An ordinary transition. The ideal scenario under which a board must select a successor CEO occurs when a successful CEO retires normally, allowing ample time to plan and prepare for the transition, in a business enjoying a strong condition with improving results.

- Scenario 2: An unexpected transition. The unexpected departure of a strong CEO from a business in a weak condition with declining results is among the worst scenarios for boards.

- Scenario 3: A termination. Another stressful scenario is one in which the board must select a successor CEO after having terminated an underperforming CEO. Businesses in these circumstances can have widely varying performance results and trends.

We will examine each of these scenarios in turn. Scenario 1 will serve as the initial case to which the other two will be compared.

ORDERLY TRANSITION

Because selecting a CEO is a board decision, the board must decide how it will organize itself to perform the task. The board usually assigns this responsibility to the nominating committee or forms a special committee to address the task. The committee must then decide on the process it will follow.

Succession Planning

The timing of when to create a succession plan is a delicate issue. A first step in succession planning is selecting a target succession date, an act sitting CEOs are often reluctant to do. The CEOs truly might not know when they will want to retire, or they might fear operating as a lame duck once they identify their plans for retirement. A proposed timeline for high-level succession planning is outlined below.

- Step 1: Two to five years in advance of an approximate changeover date. During this period, the board considers the condition and trajectory of the firm and develops a desired profile of the new CEO. A next step is for the board to determine whether there are any inside candidates for the position. If so, the board should quietly get to know the candidates and give them assignments that would test and prepare them for the job of CEO.

- Step 2: The actual succession process, including the selection of the successor. Approximately one year in advance of his or her departure date, the CEO should announce his or her retirement (although some CEOs will prefer to give much shorter notice). If a succession plan is in place, shorter notice should not create a problem. If a succession plan is not in place, however, the situation might be troublesome for the board.

- Step 3: The transition phase during which the baton is passed. The length of this phase will vary from firm to firm.

Considerations in Succession Planning

The board must make a number of potentially crucial decisions in the succession planning process. The decisions will certainly be influenced by the circumstances of the organization at the time and the individuals involved.

The Role of the CEO

A key decision in succession planning is the role the current CEO will play in the process. A successful CEO who is retiring might be looked to for a great deal of input. Such a CEO has the confidence of the board and knows the inside candidates well. In these cases, though, the CEO should be seen only as an adviser to the board, never the person making the decision. A concern the board must address is whether the CEO can remain sufficiently objective in evaluating the inside candidates. After years of concurrent service with his or her potential successors, most CEOs would find it impossible to remain impartial. For this reason, alone, a retiring CEO should not be permitted to pick his or her successor.

Inside Candidates

Naturally, the board must determine if there are inside candidates for the CEO position. Many successful companies take pride in being able to promote from within. These companies benefit from promoting an individual who is well known to the board and experienced in the business and its systems. If things are going well and continuity is desired, an insider can be a preferred option. If things are not going so well, however, and change is needed, it is often better to bring in someone from outside the company with fresh ideas and no deep ties to existing managers.

When there is more than one internal candidate, the board must devise a process by which the field will be narrowed to one. This might involve providing the candidates with a variety of assignments that prepare them better for the job of CEO, thus giving the board an opportunity to observe how well they perform. A staff executive might be given a line responsibility as a division general manager, and a line manager might be brought back to the corporate office in a senior staff position. In addition to their job assignments, the candidates might be asked to make presentations at regular board and board committee meetings.

This process would obviously require a lengthy period to play out in a meaningful way. A danger associated with such a lengthy process is the potential of creating a competitive race that becomes politicized and disruptive to the management of the business. The assessment of inside candidates must be handled very skillfully, therefore, in order to be perceived as a part of a well-executed management succession process. In order to avoid the appearance of a contest, some boards will identify the candidates, observe them in their regular roles, and make their choice very quietly and quickly. When an individual is selected from a group of candidates, those passed over frequently leave the company. This should be anticipated in the board's selection of the new leader. If such departures might create unacceptable problems, the ultimate choice of the board might need to be adjusted.

After a successor has been identified, he or she is often moved to the CEO position in a series of steps. The most common process is to have the individual first run a major division or subsidiary of the company. After a year or two as a division president, the individual might be promoted to chief operating officer (COO) and then eventually to CEO.

Going Outside
If there are no viable candidates for CEO inside the company, or if the board feels that an outsider is needed because of the situation, the board must establish a process for finding an outsider to be CEO.

If an obvious, desirable candidate is known to the board, the process can move very quickly. In these cases, the board typically appoints a director or small group of directors to approach the individual and assess his or her interest. If the candidate expresses interest, the board normally sets up private conversations designed to recruit the individual. In the case of a successful outcome, negotiations ensue over the terms of employment.

If there is no obvious outside candidate for CEO, the board must undertake a search. Frequently, this involves engaging an executive search firm. While advertising a job might be a legal requirement, the most desirable candidates might not respond to an ad. They must be sought out and recruited. This is where search firms add value, along with their ability to check references thoroughly. Absent the use of an executive search firm, the process must be run by management, usually by the senior human resources officer.

When a board finds an outside successor for the CEO position, one of its key decisions is whether to have the individual join the company as CEO or be hired into some other role with the opportunity to phase into the job. This decision will depend on the stature and experience of the individual.

Communications

An important part of the selection process is communicating progress, both inside the organization and to the public. The communication usually begins when the retirement date of the current CEO is announced, which customarily takes place 6 to 12 months in advance of the actual departure date. If there is a stated policy or tradition that the CEO retires at a given age, then all who know the CEO's age know when that date is, and the announcement of a pending retirement is no surprise. Without such a policy, or in cases of self-chosen retirement, an announcement would need to be somewhat explanatory.

When there is to be an outside successor to the CEO and a public search is to be undertaken, that plan should be announced, usually at the time that the retirement date of the current CEO is announced. If the board has identified an obvious outside successor, however, it might not announce the plan until the candidate and the board have reached an agreement.

Transition to a New CEO

When a successful CEO is retiring, it is normally useful that he or she remain affiliated with the company for six months to a year to support the new CEO. Obvious benefits of this strategy include access to the retiring CEO's institutional knowledge and smooth introduction of the new CEO by the departing CEO into important relationships both inside and outside the company. (This assumes that the departing CEO has a reservoir of goodwill to pass along.)

As noted in an earlier chapter, the board must decide whether a CEO who has been both chairman and CEO should be retained as chairman of the board for some interval after his or her retirement from the CEO position. Generally, it is best for the retiring CEO to leave the board after a reasonable transition period of no more than a year.

TRANSITION AFTER AN UNEXPECTED DEPARTURE

Scenario 2, which was briefly described earlier, is the most difficult scenario for a board. It involves the unexpected departure of a strong CEO of a business competing from a weak condition and with declining results. In general, this situation entails a CEO becoming disabled or dying unexpectedly while the company is in a weak position. A primary consideration for the board is the urgency of finding a replacement for a weak company. A similar situation arises when a CEO abruptly resigns, although the resignation might involve varying degrees of damage to the company, depending on the precipitating reasons.

In situations when a CEO departs unexpectedly, it is invaluable to the board to have a contingency succession plan already prepared. To formalize this plan, the nominating committee might ask the CEO annually to recommend a successor in the event of his or her incapacitation. The board might also have private, periodic discussions about succession, particularly during executive sessions.

In the event that the board finds the firm's succession plan acceptable, the appointed successor would be in place to be promoted. If the board determines that no insider is appropriate, the board will have to launch a search for an outsider as described above. The board will usually appoint an interim CEO to serve while the search is conducted. The interim CEO is customarily a member of management or the board, although the board sometimes turns to a consultant or retired executive from outside. As mentioned, the board as a rule does not have the luxury of pursuing a lengthy process to appoint a permanent CEO under these conditions.

TRANSITION AFTER TERMINATION

The third scenario described earlier is one in which the board terminates an underperforming CEO. In practice, such situations tend to be rare. When they do occur, the departing CEOs tend to leave fairly quickly after the decision is made to terminate employment. Underperforming lame ducks are of marginal value—if any—to the organization.

In this situation, the board again is faced with the insider versus outsider choice. The difference in this scenario is that there might be some strong feelings about the departing individual, and some managers loyal to him or her might depart as well. If the recalcitrant executives do not depart, the board might want to remove them to eliminate their negative attitudes.

Due to the need to move quickly, the board in this situation (as well as the second scenario) might tend to settle for mediocrity as a safe course. In the long run, this is not an effective strategy. The firm would be better served if the board chose to appoint someone not yet proven but appearing to have the potential to quickly grow into the job of CEO. The board then would need to be prepared for the possibility of having to act if the new CEO were incapable of effectively serving in the new position.

When the board terminates a CEO, special communications are required. In particular, it is important for the board to demonstrate its control of the situation by effectively communicating its intentions to the key managers, the rank and file employees, and the public.

THE WORKING RELATIONSHIP BETWEEN THE BOARD AND THE CEO

After the board of directors chooses the CEO, it delegates to him or her responsibility for running the business. Thus begins a hopefully productive, albeit complex, relationship. The board's role in the relationship is first to understand and approve of the CEO's strategies and plans and then to monitor the execution of those plans and to periodically evaluate the results. Finally, the board must decide whether, when, and how it should intervene. The way in which the board executes its role is crucial to the success of the relationship, and ultimately, of the business.

A board must be careful in determining its level of involvement in the running of the business. A board that crosses the line by interfering or micromanaging can undermine the effectiveness of the CEO and will find it difficult to hold the CEO accountable for poor results that it might have had a part in bringing about. On the other hand, a board that is too detached from what is happening or too passive in intervening is not carrying out its responsibilities. Board members must strive to find the right balance between these two extremes, staying proactive in carrying out their responsibilities as directors without interfering.

In finding this balance, it is of primary importance that the members of the board remain independent of the CEO. Independence requires board members to refrain from providing any paid services to the CEO or the company. Similarly, board members should not let personal friendships with the CEO interfere with carrying out their duties. Independence of board members from a CEO does not require an adversarial relationship; on the contrary, the parties must establish and develop effective ways of communicating and working together in a collaborative partnership built on mutual respect. Both parties must remember that, ultimately, the CEO is accountable to the board.

An effective management model for a board-CEO relationship should involve the following:

- Hiring an appropriate CEO for the firm. An appropriate CEO is one who shares the values of the board and organization and has the requisite abilities to run the business effectively.

- Developing mutually agreeable goals, policies, and standards of performance for the CEO with the input of the CEO.
- Aligning the interests of the board and CEO with those of the shareholders. This is done primarily through stock ownership and incentive plans.
- Agreeing on the decisions that should be brought to the board, those decisions on which the board wants to "advise and consent," and those that are delegated to the CEO. Such agreements should serve to establish a well-understood line between the responsibilities of the board and those of the CEO.
- Remaining knowledgeable about the firm's activities and performance in appropriate detail and in a timely manner and evaluating the results. Failure to have the controls and communication in place to remain knowledgeable indicates a failure on the part of the board to execute its responsibilities.
- Reacting appropriately to the results by holding management accountable and rewarding or intervening as necessary.

EVALUATING THE PERFORMANCE OF THE CEO

The evaluation of the performance of the CEO is a major responsibility of a board. In practice, it should be a continuous process of observation and interaction. In addition to assessing the CEO's performance at board and committee meetings, the board also should assess his or her performance in terms of the agreed-upon goals, standards, and time frames for achieving planned results. The missing of goals on a regular basis should raise serious questions for the board. The board usually should also have opinions about the "softer" side of a CEO's performance, including his or her style, presentation effectiveness, and relationships with the board members themselves.

Outside directors should follow the good practice of routinely meeting in executive session at the end of every board meeting. In these sessions, they should discuss any concerns they have about the CEO's performance, and the lead director should provide the CEO with appropriate feedback from these sessions.

In addition to these ongoing assessments, the board should perform a formal performance evaluation of the CEO at least annually, which should be very specific and candid. The CEO should be given an opportunity to respond to criticism and clarify any misunderstandings. This evaluation should not be a negative exercise, but one marked by open and frank conversations that provide the CEO with the feedback he or she needs to meet the board's expectations. The board should be careful to provide the CEO with positive as well as negative feedback during the annual performance evaluation, and the evaluation should also include a discussion of the CEO's compensation for the coming period of assessment, typically one year. The following chapter addresses in more detail this high-profile topic of CEO compensation.

CHAPTER 6

CEO COMPENSATION

INTRODUCTION

One of the more visible tasks a board of directors must deal with is determining the compensation of the chief executive officer (CEO) and senior managers. Management compensation must reward strong current performance and simultaneously provide incentives for similar future results. Additionally, the compensation should be structured to avoid paying premiums for average or poor performance. The task is not simple; the board wants to attract the right people, find the right alignment of their performance and shareholders' interests in both the short and long term, and use the most tax-efficient methods. Boards often worry much more about losing an obviously impressive CEO to another firm than about the less threatening possibility of some outside pressure group questioning an expansive level of CEO compensation.

Compensation of the CEO is generally administered by a compensation committee of the board of directors. The 2003 revised listing rules of the New York Stock Exchange (NYSE) and the NASDAQ address compensation committees. The NYSE rules, which are somewhat more stringent than those of the NASDAQ, require the following:

- Listed companies must have a compensation committee composed entirely of independent directors.
- The committee must have a written charter that addresses:
  - The committee's purpose and responsibilities, which include:
    - The review and approval of corporate goals and objectives relevant to CEO compensation
    - Evaluation of the CEO's performance in light of the established goals and objectives
    - Determination and approval of the CEO's compensation level based on the evaluation

- • Making recommendations to the board regarding non-CEO compensation, incentive compensation plans, and equity-based plans
- • The production of a report on executive compensation as required by the SEC to be included in the company's annual proxy statement or annual report on Form 10-K filed with the SEC
- • An annual performance evaluation of the committee
- • The rules also recommend the charter address two additional issues, which are:
  - • Committee member qualifications, member appointment and removal, committee structure and operations, and requirements for committee reporting to the board
  - • Delegating to the committee sole authority to hire and terminate a compensation consultant and to approve the firm's fees and terms

In addition to the stock exchange rules with regard to the compensation committee, the Sarbanes-Oxley Act of 2002 and revised rules of the exchanges provide other new, related requirements. Recommendations also abound from industry organizations such as the Business Roundtable, the National Association of Corporate Directors, and the Conference Board Commission on Public Trust. Many of the important new requirements are discussed in Chapter 8.

PAY FOR PERFORMANCE

Boards desire to pay CEOs and management teams for good performance. This concept might be simple, but its implementation is complicated. Different business situations, for example start-ups, growth businesses, tough industry conditions, and turnarounds, create very different compensation challenges. Performance in each instance must be determined with the situation in mind.

Similarly, the nature of the business should also be considered when assessing executive performance. One of the best performing life insurance companies, for example, does not pay incentive compensation. The company's board believes that the nuances of their industry make the measure of performance in the short term very difficult. The board feels that underwriting practices can only be measured over the very long term, and as a result, it has chosen not to provide incentives to increase policy volume that might encourage a relaxation of underwriting standards. Likewise, investment performance can best be viewed over the long term, taking into account the risks incurred. A board would not want incentives that might encourage greater risk taking, the results of which would not be apparent for many years.

CONSIDERATIONS IN SETTING COMPENSATION

A compensation committee should consider many factors in setting a CEO's compensation. Important factors include the following:

- The value of the CEO to the company. This is, by far, the most important consideration, yet difficult to quantify.
- The company's capacity to compensate the CEO, reflecting its size and profitability. (See Exhibits 6-1 and 6-2 for illustrations of the effects of company size on average CEO compensation.)
- Absolute performance of the company over some time period based on indicators reflecting universal financial standards.
- Relative performance of the company compared to industry comparable companies.
- Achievement of nonfinancial goals, particularly strategic ones.
- External parity with other comparable companies' CEO compensation packages. Companies must also consider prevailing trends in the marketplace. As a rule, if the company wants to attract and retain outstanding executives, it must provide better-than-average compensation unless there are some unusual circumstances that tie the executives to the company.
- Internal parity. Boards should consider the relationship between the compensation of the CEO and that of the rest of the management team. Frequently, the CEO is paid twice as much as the next senior officer. (See Exhibits 6-1 and 6-2.)

Generally, boards attempt to link pay to performance by putting a significant percentage of the CEO's compensation at-risk. How much is put at-risk, with the at-risk component not guaranteed but instead linked to the achievement of specified performance targets, depends on the board's philosophy and the nature of the business. The board, through the compensation committee, should strive to align executive compensation with the achievement of the business strategy.

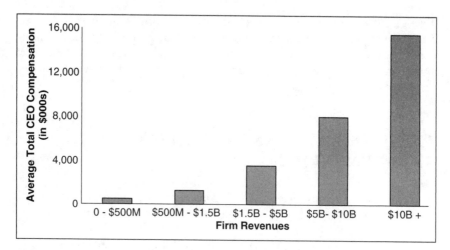

EXHIBIT 6-1 Total Average CEO Compensation in Relation to Company Size—
Year 2000 (*Source*: Company Proxy Statements Data from an Unpublished Study.)

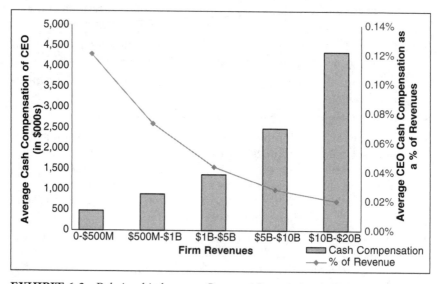

EXHIBIT 6-2 Relationship between Company Revenues and CEO Salaries—Year
2000 (*Source*: Company Proxy Statements Data from an Unpublished Study.)

SAMPLE STUDY OF EXTERNAL PARITY OF CEO COMPENSATION

In order to calibrate for discussions of prevailing levels of CEO and executive compensation, the relevant board committees should undertake
periodic studies of compensation levels and components in a peer group

Component of Compensation	Company Performing Study	Marketplace Median	Marketplace 75th percentile	Company Versus Median	Company Versus 75th percentile
Base salary	$450,000	$533,000	$630,000	-16%	-29%
Bonus target 60% of salary	$270,000	$270,000	$420,000	0%	-36%
Total cash	$720,000	$803,000	$1,050,000	-10%	-31%
Equity	$125,000	$797,000	$1,450,000	-84%	-91%
Total compensation	$845,000	$1,600,000	$2,450,000	-47%	-66%

Figures should be considered in the context of the company's performance relative to that of the comparison companies.

EXHIBIT 6-3   Sample Study of External Parity of CEO Compensation

of companies. It is presumed that the company competes with these peer companies for customers as well as top management talent; thus, the peer firms reasonably represent the marketplace to which the company should compare itself. A sample of one company's study of external parity for CEO compensation is shown in Exhibit 6-3.

As noted in the exhibit, compensation figures should be considered in the context of the company's performance relative to that of the comparison companies. Thus, if the company performing the study underperformed the marketplace of peer companies on several key financial or performance indicators, one would expect its CEO to be paid less than those of better-performing firms. This observation highlights the need for compensation committees also to perform analyses benchmarking the performance of the company against that of a relevant peer group. Benchmarking studies of firm and industry performance should encompass numerous absolute measures (e.g., net income) as well as ratios and growth rates (e.g., return on equity and growth rate of net income). Compensation committee members should give special emphasis to those measures relevant and important to attaining and sustaining competitive advantage and increasing shareholder value. As one might guess, the task of setting CEO compensation is complex and requires considerable effort on the part of compensation committee members.

THE CEO COMPENSATION PACKAGE

Regardless of the difficulties involved, boards must fashion compensation packages for their CEOs. A CEO compensation package generally consists of the following:

- Base salary
- Short-term incentives
- Long-term incentives
- Fringe benefits
- Perquisites, or perks

Incentives might include cash bonuses and stock options, grants, and ownership plans. In addition to determining the level of compensation, the board has to decide on the mix among the many forms of compensation.

BASE SALARY

Base salary is a guaranteed, fixed cash amount paid to an executive. In some companies with outstanding performance, the base salary is as low as 10 to 15 percent of total compensation. There are even a few cases where CEOs receive no base salary, only at-risk compensation. On the other hand, in companies with weak performance results, a base salary frequently will account for 50 to 100 percent of the total compensation. This situation is not due to discrepancies in the size of the salaries, but to determinations that the executives are not performing sufficiently well to earn substantial incentives. There are few companies that do not use incentive compensation in some form. Exhibit 6-4 illustrates the shifting proportions of salary and bonus in CEO compensation based on the level of compensation.

SHORT-TERM INCENTIVES

Short-term incentives are bonuses paid for outstanding performance. They can be paid in cash and/or company stock. The criteria for earning short-term incentives generally include achieving the corporate strategy and goals. Most companies use several performance measures in determining short-term incentive awards and often establish threshold levels of performance that the firm must achieve in order for executives to earn short-term incentives. The most frequently used measures include:

- Profits and earnings per share
- Revenue growth
- Return on investment measures, including economic value added (EVA), which is a sophisticated form of measuring return against the cost of capital
- Cash flow
- Strategic measures, such as market share

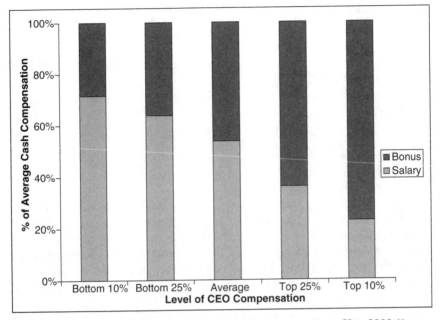

EXHIBIT 6-4   Proportion of Total CEO Cash Compensation—Year 2000 (*Source:* Company Proxy Statements Data from an Unpublished Study.)

Many companies also use nonfinancial measures related to customer or employee satisfaction, quality, and safety, among others. Some companies might also offer incentive pay for the completion of a given important project. Certain companies pay incentives for performance improvements when the threshold targets are not yet being met.

LONG-TERM INCENTIVES

Long-term incentives are the most difficult to design properly but are the principal means by which the sought-after alignment between the interests of managers and shareholders is accomplished. Ironically, these incentives are also the instruments through which most of the flagrant abuses in compensation have taken place.

Long-term incentive approaches include the following:

- Stock options
- Restricted shares
- Required stock purchases
- Stock appreciation rights (SARs)
- Cash

Stock Options

A number of prescribed events must occur for an executive to reap a financial gain from awarded stock options. The key events in order of occurrence are as follows:

- The grant of the option
- Vesting of the option
- Exercise of the option
- Holding of the stock
- Sale of the stock

A straightforward stock option grants the holder the right to purchase a specified number of shares of the firm's stock at a stipulated price (known as the strike price)—usually the market price at the time the option was issued—for the term of the option. The term of an option is specified and is usually 10 years or less. The awarding of the total number of shares is often staggered over time, with the total number awarded vesting gradually, year by year. *Vesting* is the technical term for the granting of the right to exercise the option, that is, the stock options actually becoming the property of the holder. To exercise an option, the holder purchases the stock at the specified price. Typically, the option is forfeited if the individual leaves the company (except through death, disability, or retirement) or simply allows the option to expire.

As an example, if a board grants an option to an employee to purchase 1000 shares of stock at $10 per share for 10 years, and in that time the stock price rises to $50 per share, the holder can earn a pretax profit of $40 a share, or $40,000 by exercising the option, purchasing the shares for $10 per share, and selling the shares for $50 per share. In large companies, a grant of options to the CEO for a small percentage of the outstanding shares can, in effect, amount to a very large number of shares for the CEO, and consequently the opportunity to earn substantial profits. Many senior executives accumulate options to purchase hundreds of thousands of shares.

Boards often confer stock options as a lump-sum, front-end grant when a key person is hired or promoted. Typically, boards also grant options annually. Acceptable levels of stock options outstanding can be as high as 10 to 15 percent of the total number of shares outstanding. Above that threshold, stockholders often get uncomfortable. If a firm aims to stay within the 10 to 15 percent range, annual grants, as a rule, should average about 1 to 2 percent of the total shares outstanding.

An advantage of stock options is that they provide a simple means of linking compensation to performance. With options, the CEO's incentive is tied directly to the stock price, so when shareholders prosper, management does as well. Straightforward stock option grants have some shortcomings, though, which many companies try to mitigate through the addition of terms and conditions. Two common limitations placed on executive stock options are performance-based vesting and stipulated holding periods after the option has been exercised.

Because a company's stock price can vary for reasons other than those related to management's performance, the vesting of the ownership of an option may be based on performance criteria that are more under the control of the receiving manager. These criteria may be long-term versions of the short-term incentive criteria discussed earlier, such as minimum targets for EPS, revenue growth, and ROE. This restriction is known as performance-based vesting.

One of the more common abuses of options has been for managers to "pump and dump" the stock. In these cases, executives run the stock up by some means in the short run and immediately thereafter sell their shares. A solution to this exploitation is to require that executives hold the stock for some period of time after they exercise the option. This stipulation, however, creates a liquidity issue for most option holders. In order to exercise an option with a holding period, the holder must have cash to purchase the stock. Because executives often do not have the cash required, in the past, companies would lend employees the money to purchase the stock. Such loans to directors and executives are now prohibited under the Sarbanes-Oxley Act.

Instead, executives now sometimes sell back shares they already own to exercise options in lieu of purchasing the shares with cash. For example, if a manager owned 1000 shares worth $20,000 ($20 per share), and had an option to purchase 2000 shares at a price of $10 per share (total price $20,000), he or she could effectively trade in the 1000 owned shares for the 2000 new shares worth $40,000.

Another drawback of using stock options as compensation is that they only deliver rewards when there is appreciation in the price of the company stock. Options that are under water, that is, those for which the strike price is above the current market share price, can be demoralizing. When companies are going through difficult times in a tough economic or competitive environment, managers might be working harder and under greater stress than in good times. The board must turn to other means of incentive under these circumstances.

An important decision for the board is how deep into the organization stock options should be granted. Two common approaches span the spectrum of this issue. One approach is to use options only for high-level executives who can make a long-term impact on the business. The other approach is to spread them deeply into the organization to create a culture of an employee-owned company. Both methods have been employed successfully, although the former is probably the more widely used technique.

One of the most controversial aspects of options is determining their value, especially as related to the issue of companies expensing options on their financial reports. A company cannot know with certainty the ultimate cost of an option at the time of issue without knowing the price of the stock at the time of exercise. If the stock does not appreciate in value, there is no "cost" to the company associated with the option.

Values are indeed assigned to options, as demonstrated by the market for options in publicly traded securities. The fact that options have an intrinsic value, however, does not mean there is a current cost to the company granting the option. The option has a potential, unknowable future cost, in the form of the dilution of shareholders' ownership if the market value of the stock appreciates. The "cost" is the allocated portion of future market capitalization given to the option holder. (This assumes that the market appreciation would have occurred even if no options had been given.)

The underlying economic assumption of granting options, though, is that the recipients will create incremental market value for the shareholders that otherwise would not have been realized. The shareholders decide the percentage of that incremental value they are willing to share with those who will help create the increase when shareholders vote to authorize options.

It should be noted that most options are classified as *nonqualifying*, meaning that they do not qualify for capital gains treatment in regard to taxes. Gains will be taxed as ordinary income at the time the option is exercised. Qualified options, however, defer income taxes on the gain until they are sold. Because of a number of restrictions regarding allowable grant levels, nonqualified options are used more commonly.

Performance Share Grants or Restricted Stock

Many companies prefer grants of restricted shares based on performance over stock options. Grants of restricted shares involve giving a CEO a certain number of shares of stock, which then vest over a specified period, usually three to five years, predicated on the CEO's staying with the company and/or achieving long-term performance goals. If vesting is based on continued employment, the shares serve as golden handcuffs, enticing the CEO to stay at the company. In some cases, though, stock grants are used as forms of short-term incentives, particularly to deliver a portion of the CEO's bonus in stock rather than cash.

Restricted stock grants are attractive in that they require fewer shares than options to provide a given dollar value reward to the CEO. This advantage results from the fact that stock options require the executive to purchase the shares (albeit at a price below the current market price), while grants require no payments to the firm.

A disadvantage of stock grants is that performance shares are taxable as income at the time of vesting. If a company were to give a CEO a grant of 4500 restricted shares that vested immediately with a market value of $45,000, the executive would likely have a tax liability in the range of $20,000, depending on his or her tax bracket. Because CEOs normally hold company stock rather than sell it, demonstrating their confidence in the firm, this tax liability may sometimes seem excessive.

For example, when CEOs hold onto stock whose market price tumbles, they must pay the tax liability on the value of the stock at the time they received it regardless of how quickly or far the price declines. Owning stock whose market price can go up or down, however, and for which an executive has had to put up cash for taxes, should give that individual a real stake in the fate of the company, which is generally considered a positive attribute of an incentive plan.

When companies grant performance-based stock, executives frequently must earn the shares over a three- to five-year period. Some companies will have a single plan in effect for the entire term of the stock grant, while other firms may employ multiple plans with overlapping terms, adding a new three- or five-year plan each year. In these cases, performance targets are established, and when met, trigger the awarding of specified levels of stock.

Stock Ownership

Some companies require that directors and key managers build up specified minimum ownership positions through the purchase of stock. For executives, the amount of stock required is often in proportion to their salaries. Stock ownership has the benefit of aligning the interests of the directors and executives with those of the shareholders, as the directors and executives become shareholders themselves.

Cash Awards

Some companies use cash as long-term incentives for CEOs. Among the purposes of using cash is the financing, at least in part, of CEO stock purchases and income tax payments related to stock grants and the exercise of options.

FRINGE BENEFITS AND PERQUISITES

Executives normally receive the standard fringe benefits of paid holidays, vacation, life insurance, and long-term disability and health care coverage, although sometimes at more generous levels than lower-level employees. There are, however, a whole set of benefits and perks that tend to be reserved for higher-level executives. They include supplemental executive retirement plans (SERPs), voluntary deferred compensation plans, memberships in clubs, car allowances, and use of corporate or leased aircraft. In pursuing dual levels of benefits, many companies have created a privileged class. Firms justify this duality by attributing the additional benefits to trying to make the demanding, stressful life of a corporate executive more comfortable and efficient. Such perks can be justified to a point, but in some cases are carried to excess.

CONTRACTS

Senior executives are often given contracts that include severance agreements and change of control protection. The severance agreements are essentially passages spelling out how long and how much an executive will be paid after termination. Noncompete clauses, which bar the executives from working in the industry for a specified period, are also usually a part of such agreements.

Change of control provisions provide executives with protection in the event of losing their jobs as a result of the sale of the company, or any other event resulting in a change of control. These provisions also usually trigger instant vesting of all options and restricted shares. Severance and change-of-control provisions are intended to protect the interests of honest executives who have faithfully served the company. Unfortunately, there have been many instances where nonperforming executives have walked away with large sums when they might, in fact, have deliberately triggered the change of control.

SUMMARY

As investors and observers review the complex relationships between boards of directors, representing shareholders, and CEOs, presumably representing themselves, there is a continuing debate as to how much compensation is too much. Instances in which CEOs have been enriched to the extent of even hundreds of millions of dollars remind us that the best-designed systems for CEO compensation are capable of producing unintended consequences. Regardless of the absolute level of the CEO's compensation over some time period, the board, the company's shareholders, and the world at large will look at this compensation in terms of the incremental market value of the company's shares created during the relevant time period and beyond. Only the shareholders themselves can answer the question as to the fairness of the CEO's compensation—and then only in the context of the gains (or losses) that accrued to the shareholders during the relevant period, as well as those that were set in motion for the future.

C H A P T E R   7

THE BOARD'S ROLE IN MANAGEMENT

INTRODUCTION

Corporate governance is more than an effective legal process; it must also embrace the aim of fulfilling the purpose of the organization and achieving its goals. The aim of effective corporate governance should be to create a business that can sustain success over the long run.

As noted in the previous chapter, primary actions in the cycle of corporate governance encompass the board's hiring an appropriate CEO and then delegating the responsibility for managing the business to him or her. To fulfill its responsibilities, however, the board must remain active in the affairs of the enterprise.

BOARD RELATIONSHIPS

An active board of directors engages in numerous relationships, both internally and externally. Several of these relationships, which are major determinants of the board's relative effectiveness, are discussed below.

RELATIONSHIPS BETWEEN INDIVIDUAL MEMBERS

While the individual relationships between board members vary, with some naturally closer than others, effective boards are characterized by the respect and trust their members demonstrate for one another. It is not usual for members of strong boards to develop personal as well as professional friendships. The ability of boards to function effectively as a group, however, is often severely disrupted when cliques form or when one or more directors are not trusted or respected because of suspect motives or dysfunctional behavior. Nominating committees must keep in mind

69

the issue of interpersonal relationships among board members when they seek to add new personalities to the board.

RELATIONSHIPS AS A GROUP

Individual relationships among board members naturally meld into a group culture. Effective boards seek to have meetings marked by open and honest conversations that aim to solicit a range of good ideas from the participants. Members should welcome spirited debate during the discussions, but when a decision is reached, all must be willing to support it. Regular analyses of failings or shortcomings should be undertaken and should not endeavor to assign blame, but rather resemble unemotional autopsies seeking to understand what happened in order to learn from the experience. Members must remember that the board can act only as a body. No single member of the board has the authority to act individually on behalf of the board, except as authorized by the full board.

THE LEADERSHIP

Effective boards are well led. Usually, one or two leader-members are responsible for creating agendas for and facilitating the discussion in regular board meetings. Some boards regularly rotate leadership roles based on the alignment of topics under discussion and the individual expertise of board members. Good leaders strive not to impose their views, but rather to ensure that all views are heard and discussions move efficiently toward the best resolution of the issues being discussed.

RELATIONSHIP WITH THE CEO

As noted in the last chapter, the relationship between the CEO and the board is vital to creating effective governance and should be based on mutual trust and respect. This relationship should also aim to maintain a balance between the independence of the board and the CEO and the collaboration necessary for them to work toward the best decisions for the organization. Typically, the CEO is a great deal more knowledgeable about the operations and affairs of the business than the board, and consequently, he or she must be skilled in providing the board with the information necessary to do its job in a timely and efficient manner.

DIRECTORS' KNOWLEDGE OF THE BUSINESS

In order to engage in meaningful discussions and analyses, board members must know or understand the business with reasonable proficiency.

One of the key management responsibilities of a board is to decide, with management's input, the businesses in which it will compete. The goal is to select businesses that have attractive characteristics and in which the company can compete effectively. If a company consists of a number of businesses, its corporate structure must also be determined. Often, the multibusiness firm is organized as a holding company operating through decentralized divisions or subsidiaries that report to a central parent organization.

At a high level, knowing the business means understanding the nature of the business at a conceptual level, which encompasses understanding the maturity and structure of the industry and the company's market position within the industry. It also includes understanding the forces that shape the competitive environment, which have been made well known by strategist Michael Porter, including ease of entry, the power of buyers and suppliers, the threat of substitutes, and the rivalry among existing firms.

Directors also must understand the business concept or concepts. In every business, there is (or should be) an underlying logic to the way it approaches the marketplace. If all of the competitors employ the same business concept, they must compete on the effectiveness with which they execute that concept. Real breakthroughs come when a business creates a new concept. Some classic examples of such breakthroughs include Dell's move to sell computers made on demand directly to the consumer; Southwest Airlines' low-cost formula; and Nucor Steel's establishing scrap-melting minimills as legitimate competitors in the steel industry. All of these strategies created differentiation among the firms in their industries and propelled the innovative companies to rapid growth.

At a fundamental level, knowing the business also requires an understanding of the key customers and their needs, and, more specifically, which of those needs the business is attempting to serve. Understanding the needs of the customers leads to an effective business concept, which in turn requires an understanding of the skills or competencies and resources required to support the chosen strategy.

A competency is a set of organizational capabilities that are needed to function in a given business. They can be further defined as the following:

- Core competencies. Those competencies that are central to the successful implementation of the selected strategy.
- Distinctive competencies. Those competencies that set the business apart from its competitors, generally because it performs them better than others.

In the same vein, the nature of the business and its strategy and growth rate drive the need for resources of all kinds: people and their skills, facilities and technologies, and capital. For effective performance, the required resources must be obtained in responsible ways, usually well in advance of their need.

Among the important judgments directors must make is the adequacy of the competencies and resources of the business to pursue a given strategy recommended by management. If the competencies and resources are inadequate, the board must assess the costs and risks of obtaining those that the firm lacks.

Also fundamental to understanding and supporting a business's strategy is sound knowledge of the competitors, including who they are and what their strategies, competencies, and resources entail. A comparison of the competitors' positioning in the industry as well as their strengths and weaknesses is a beneficial step for a firm in devising or confirming its strategy.

Looking inward, a board should strive for a reasonable level of understanding of the systems and structures employed in the business's primary functional areas, including product design and marketing, production or operations management, finance, human resources, and often research and development. It is particularly important that the directors understand the business model, which explains how the business will make a profit and how it is to be capitalized.

Finally, directors need to have some awareness of what the future might hold. They need to understand the driving forces affecting the competitive environment, the trends of those forces, and the impact they might have on the business. Some strategists prefer to label these issues opportunities for and threats to the business.

Naturally, it might prove difficult for a director from outside the business's industry to understand completely the complexities and details of the many facets of a firm's competitive environment and strategic response. The more the directors understand, however, the more effective they will be in their roles, for it is this understanding that creates the context for their work and decisions as directors.

THE GOALS OF THE CORPORATION

After a board has selected a good business, hired an effective CEO, and built a solid understanding of the business, it must address the question of setting goals for the organization. Generally, this is very much an iterative process, led by the CEO working with the board.

Goal-setting and benchmarking were discussed earlier in the context of CEO compensation and incentives. As a review, financial results serve as the key indicator of performance. There is no single answer, though, to the question of which metrics indicate the status of financial performance.

A goal of management should be for the company to earn a return on investment that reflects the risks inherent in and the cost of capital of the business, along with the goals of the shareholders. The board should establish a standard return-on-equity goal, considering, if relevant, the average of all of the businesses in the company portfolio, both current and historically, and the returns of peer companies. If the industry returns, as evidenced by peer-company performance, do not compare favorably with broader market returns, the board must grasp that it is in a below-average industry and adjust its strategies accordingly.

A company can focus on a variety of measures to improve and motivate change in its return on investment. These might include both absolute measures (such as sales dollars) or ratios and growth rates (such as the growth rate of sales). The approach of specifying quantifiable goals that are within management's control and linking rewards to their achievement is an extremely effective method of focusing management on desired results. Growth of earnings, in particular, is a consistently desirable goal, for as a rule it drives the price of the stock. Growth of the top line, i.e., sales growth, is a logical first step toward growth of the bottom line, i.e., growth of earnings.

In growing industries, businesses should find ways to participate in the inherent growth, either through internally generated volume or acquisitions. As an industry matures, though, growth typically slows, and to achieve notable organic growth businesses must take market share from competitors, which is a more difficult challenge. Under circumstances of slower sales growth, growth in earnings can be attained for a period by concentrating on efficiencies and margins. If growth of a successful company stalls for an extended period, it must respond by finding ways to reenergize its growth. When its fortunes remain down, management, with appropriate board approval and support, must engineer a turnaround or eventually exit the business.

RISK MANAGEMENT

Directors must also concern themselves with managing the risk associated with the business. One obvious aspect of risk management is ensuring that the business carries adequate insurance coverage to protect its assets in the event of some accident, natural disaster, court ruling, or liability. Risk management goes beyond these conventional risks, though, to include the risks inherent in the operations of the business itself.

Economic cycles, failures of major customers, and new, disruptive technologies, for example, could trigger substantial declines in revenues. Reduced cash flow as a result of reduced revenues and/or increased costs could expose the business to the possible inability to meet bank covenants or cover interest payments on debt, resulting in default. Corporate scandal, government regulation, consumer boycott...the list of additional potentially crippling events is lengthy. A board should attempt to anticipate a range of possible outcomes and judiciously prepare for the various scenarios that it cannot avoid or mitigate. Boards begin this task by asking the appropriate questions of management and verifying plans to identify and respond to risks to the business.

FULFILLING DUTIES

In Chapter 2, we addressed the primary duties of directors. They include:

- Fiduciary duty
- Duty of loyalty and the duty of fair dealing
- Duty of care
- Duty not to entrench
- Duty of supervision

It is in carrying out its work that a board and each individual director either fulfills or violates these duties. Each time the directors take an action, they should ask whether there is a conflict of interest; whether they are acting in the best interests of their shareholders and other stakeholders; and whether they are doing so conscientiously based on the best information and advice available to them.

EXECUTION

The work of a director is time-consuming and encompasses collaboration with other directors, the CEO, and other key managers. Good directors dedicate the time required to do the job well, both in and out of the boardroom. Strong directors prepare for board and committee meetings, doing their homework to understand and process the information supplied to them by the CEO and management. Much of an effective board's work is carried out within its committees, where there is opportunity to delve into important issues in much more detail than can be done at full board meetings. Ideally the directors move in circles that are relevant to the business and seek out conversations, experiences, and readings that broaden their understanding of the major issues facing or affecting the business.

In order to be effective, directors must make a concerted effort to understand the activities of their business and its industry. Delegation without controls in place to ensure that directors are appropriately briefed results in abdication, potentially with disastrous results. A prerequisite for effective control is the setting of sound goals or standards against which the actual performance of the business can be compared.

Internal control systems should report information about critical successes and failures up the management chain and to the board in appropriate detail and a timely fashion. Good directors do not depend solely on the formal reporting systems, however. They also spend time talking with the CEO and other key managers to get their views of situations and interpretations of relevant information. When possible, directors should informally observe and listen to others who might convey different perspectives, including customers, employees, competitors, and suppliers. Directors should seek open and honest feedback, assessing whether messages are positive and consistent from all of the information channels. Good directors must be willing to uncover potential shortcomings and problems and be persistent in unearthing relevant details.

When things are going well, fulfilling the role of director can seem straightforward. Interestingly, when there is a crisis, issues often come into focus rapidly and a board can mobilize itself to resolve them. The greatest challenge to the board's effectiveness, however, frequently occurs when there is gradual decline over some longer time period. The changes can be subtle, and once they are detected, boards have a tendency to wait to see if they continue. Knowing when to intervene and confront crucial issues is an essential capability for directors and requires the board to be aware of what is truly taking place.

MAKING DIFFICULT DECISIONS

A vital responsibility of directors is to make difficult decisions when they are called for. Such decisions take many forms; some infrequent yet often difficult decisions include deciding whether to sell the core business or line of business, not to issue or file reports because their contents are suspect, to self-report on a regulatory violation, to accept or reject a hostile takeover bid, and to close or move a large facility and initiate substantial layoffs of employees.

A common decision effective boards must make is determining how to deal with board members who are not carrying out their responsibilities well or who have committed some dereliction of duty. Boards typically find the most serious transgressions the easiest to handle. Mediocrity and annoying behavior, however, can be more difficult for the board to address.

Further difficult decisions regularly involve disagreements with the CEO. Such decisions might take the form of telling the CEO that he or she must take certain actions or that he or she may not pursue a proposed course of action. When these kinds of disagreements surface with a CEO, a danger arises that the board will cross the line into micromanaging the business, which creates numerous problems of its own. When the board requires management to implement a specific decision or plan, it might find it difficult to hold the CEO accountable if desirable results fail to materialize. Conversely, a difficult decision might encompass choosing to support the CEO in a difficult time, whether work related or personal.

Finally, the most difficult decision most boards face is that of deciding to change the CEO. A change in CEO may be effected by variety of means, including termination, failure to renew a contract, and resignation or retirement following a mutual agreement that it is time for a CEO to step down.

When should a board intervene in the management of a company and terminate the CEO? The answer is when the board loses confidence in the CEO or he or she is guilty of some wrongdoing. Loss of confidence can be traced to any one or combination of the following causes:

- Board members feel the strategy proposed is inappropriate for the firm at the time.

- Board members feel the CEO and his or her team have not been (or will not be) able to implement the strategy effectively.

- The CEO does not see or understand a problem or opportunity, even after it is pointed out to him or her, including inarguably poor results.

- The CEO sees the problem or opportunity but does not develop a plan for dealing with it in a timely fashion.

- The CEO has a plan to deal with a problem or opportunity but is unable to execute it.

- The CEO lacks candor or honesty in dealing with the board.

In such cases, the board may seek to remove the CEO and look for stronger leadership to carry out the perceived superior strategy or plan of action. In order to act with confidence, the board must keep itself informed about all aspects of the company's operations. If board members doubt the CEO's plans, abilities, or integrity, they must take the necessary steps to inform themselves and prepare for action. The shareholders deserve nothing less, and board members have committed themselves to responsibly carrying out this duty.

The board's role in management of the company involves many responsibilities, including the important task of maintaining a healthy relationship with the CEO. This complex relationship requires both independence and a mutual commitment to work toward the achievement of common goals in the interests of the shareholders. The board also has a duty to remain informed about the operations of the business as well as its competitive environment in good times and bad, for it is this foundation of knowledge on which it must base its many important decisions and actions.

CHAPTER 8

NEW REQUIREMENTS: SARBANES-OXLEY ACT AND STOCK EXCHANGE RULES

INTRODUCTION

The corporate scandals of recent years have resulted in a wave of new regulations and legislation. Most prominent among them is the Sarbanes-Oxley Act of 2002 (often referred to as SOX). This Act addresses perceived weaknesses in auditing, reporting, and corporate governance of U.S. public companies and has been hailed as the most dramatic change to federal securities laws in over 50 years. In combination with related actions and provisions from the Securities and Exchange Commission (SEC), which administers the laws set forth in the act, and rule changes from the major stock exchanges, notably the New York Stock Exchange (NYSE) and the Nasdaq Stock Exchange (NASDAQ), the Sarbanes-Oxley Act has established enhanced regulations for public company governance and reporting requirements.

The rule changes at the NYSE and NASDAQ came in response to a request from the Chairman of the SEC, who asked the exchanges to examine their listing standards with an emphasis on all those related to corporate governance. In response, the NYSE and the National Association of Securities Dealers (NASD) through its subsidiary, the Nasdaq Stock Market, Inc., filed corporate governance reform proposals with the SEC. Specifically, in August of 2002, the NYSE filed the NYSE Corporate Governance Proposal to amend its listed company manual. In October of 2002, the NASD, through the Nasdaq, filed a proposed rule change known as the Nasdaq Independent Director Proposal. Both proposals were subsequently amended and eventually approved by the SEC.

THE NEW REQUIREMENTS

The following section provides a summary of and brief commentary on important new and revised requirements for boards, committees, and individual directors of publicly traded companies that emanated from the Sarbanes-Oxley Act and the changes to the NYSE and NASDAQ rules. These sources overlap on many requirements and frequently provide similar direction with slight variation in language. As a result, the summary below is intended to capture the general intent of the important new and revised requirements rather than the precise wording or specific directions of the various source documents. Furthermore, not all of the details of the Sarbanes-Oxley Act or the NYSE and NASDAQ rule changes are high-lighted here, nor are exemptions fully addressed. Additionally, the SEC continues to issue rules related to the enactment of the provisions of the Sarbanes-Oxley Act.

Among the provisions of the Sarbanes-Oxley Act that do not directly apply to activities of directors of public companies are the establishment of the Public Accounting Oversight Board and the requirements that all public accounting firms register with and supply information to this newly established body. This board is charged with establishing standards address-ing auditing, quality control, ethics, and independence relating to the preparation of audit reports for public companies. Sarbanes-Oxley also addresses penalties and broadened sanctions for corporate and criminal fraud as well as provisions for increasing the independence of firms that audit the financial statements of public companies.

STRENGTHENING CORPORATE RESPONSIBILITY THROUGH GOVERNANCE

LISTED COMPANIES MUST HAVE A MAJORITY OF INDEPENDENT DIRECTORS

The premise of this rule proposed by both of the exchanges is that the representatives of the shareholders should be, for the most part, inde-pendent of the management they oversee. Members of management who also are directors are likely to have a conflict of interest in evaluating their own performance and in taking any necessary actions with regard to poor performance.

There are many facets of the definition of an independent director. For example, the NYSE rules stipulate that a director is deemed to be independent when the board determines that he or she is not an employee of the company and has no material relationship with the company, either directly or as a partner, shareholder, or officer of an organization that has a relationship with the company.

Independence also requires a three-year "cooling-off" or "look-back" period for former employees of the company or of its independent auditor, persons having received substantial payment from the company, and former employees of any company that has done a threshold level of business with the company. This three-year period applies as well to former employees of any company whose compensation committee includes an officer of the listed company, and to immediate family members of any of the above.

In addition to requiring the majority of the board to be independent, the NYSE rules require that the Audit, Nominating/Corporate Governance, and Compensation Committees be composed solely of independent directors.

NONMANAGEMENT OR INDEPENDENT DIRECTORS MUST MEET WITHOUT MANAGEMENT IN REGULARLY SCHEDULED EXECUTIVE SESSIONS

The purpose of this stock-exchange requirement is to give the nonmanagement directors an opportunity to discuss privately the performance of management and any other sensitive issues and to serve as an effective check on management. The premise is that regular meetings of nonmanagement directors will promote open discussion and foster better communication and inquiry.

THE AUDIT COMMITTEE IS RESPONSIBLE FOR THE FISCAL INTEGRITY OF THE CORPORATION

There are many important requirements of the audit committee. Sarbanes-Oxley prohibits national securities exchanges (stock exchanges) from listing the stock of a company unless each member of the company's audit committee is independent. Furthermore, the act outlines the purpose of this vital committee as overseeing the accounting and financial reporting process of the company and audits of the financial statements.

The NYSE requires that all members of the audit committee must be or become financially literate, while NASDAQ maintains that all members must be able to read and understand fundamental financial statements at the time of their appointment. Furthermore, both exchanges require that at least one audit committee member has some specified financial expertise or experience, and Sarbanes-Oxley requires the reporting of whether the audit committee has at least one member who qualifies as a "financial expert," and if not, why not.

Sarbanes-Oxley also requires that the audit committee has sole responsibility for selection and oversight of the company's auditors and that it must preapprove auditing as well as any significant, allowed, nonaudit services. The auditing firm must report directly to the audit committee.

Sarbanes-Oxley further requires the audit committee to establish procedures for receiving and responding to complaints received by the company regarding accounting or auditing matters and to confidential and anonymous submissions by employees regarding questionable accounting or auditing matters. In fact, Sarbanes-Oxley makes it illegal for publicly traded companies to retaliate against employees who provide evidence of fraud or SEC violations.

Other important requirements of the audit committee established in the NYSE rules include that the audit committee:

- Review the independent auditor's work at least annually
- Discuss the company's annual audited financial statements and quarterly financial statements with management and the independent auditor
- Discuss the company's earnings press releases as well as financial information and earnings guidance provided to analysts and rating agencies
- Discuss policies with respect to risk assessment and risk management
- Have separate, periodic meetings with management, internal auditors, and the independent auditors
- Review with the independent auditors any audit problems or difficulties, with management's response
- Report regularly to the board

ENHANCED FINANCIAL DISCLOSURES

THE CEO AND THE CFO MUST CERTIFY THE FINANCIAL RESULTS

In a move to bring personal accountability to the act of financial reporting, Sarbanes-Oxley requires that the CEO and the CFO must certify the full and accurate reporting of financial results in each annual or quarterly report. More specifically, the CEO and CFO must certify, based on their knowledge, the following:

- The report does not contain any untrue statement of a material fact or does not omit to state a material fact.

- The financial statement and disclosures fairly represent in all material respects the financial condition and results of operations of the company.
- The signing officers are responsible for and have evaluated and reported on the effectiveness of internal controls.

The act also stipulates that certifying officers will face penalties of up to $1,000,000 in fines and/or up to 10 years' imprisonment for "knowing" violations and up to $5,000,000 in fines and/or up to 20 years' imprisonment for "willful" and "knowing" violations.

IT IS ILLEGAL FOR OFFICERS AND DIRECTORS TO FRAUDULENTLY INFLUENCE AN INDEPENDENT AUDITOR

In its role of independently auditing a company's financial results, a public accounting firm is expected to function without conflict of interest or influence from any interested parties within the company. Such influence would compromise the independence of the auditor's report. To protect the outside auditor's independence, Sarbanes-Oxley makes it unlawful for any officer or director, or others acting under their direction, to fraudulently influence, coerce, manipulate, or mislead an independent auditor engaged in auditing the company's financials.

COMPANY CODES OF ETHICS

Sarbanes-Oxley requires that companies disclose in SEC filings whether they have a code of ethics for senior financial officials and any changes in or waivers from such codes. NYSE rules require all listed companies to adopt and disclose a code of business conduct and ethics for directors, officers, and employees, and promptly disclose any waivers of the code for directors or executive officers. Finally, the NASDAQ rules require each listed company to adopt a code of conduct applicable to all directors, officers, and employees, and to make the code publicly available. The code would be required to comply with the Sarbanes-Oxley definition of a code of ethics and to include an enforcement mechanism. Waivers of the code for directors or executive officers must be approved by the board and disclosed within five days.

ACCELERATED REPORTING OF AND NEW RESTRICTIONS ON TRADING BY INSIDERS

There have always been limitations on trading by directors and other insiders in terms of the amount and timing of trades and the requirements for related reporting. Insiders traditionally have not been permitted to trade during periods in which they had information not available to others. A new rule of Sarbanes-Oxley addresses directors, officers, and principal stockholders (owners of more than 10 percent of any class of any equity security) and requires that any trades must be reported to the SEC by the end of the second business day after the day on which the transaction was executed. An additional rule prohibits insider trades during pension fund blackout periods. Pension blackout periods are periods of more than three days during which a majority of participants are not permitted to change their choice of retirement plans. Under this rule, directors and executive officers are prohibited from buying, selling, or trading company stock during blackout periods.

FUTURE PERSONAL LOANS TO DIRECTORS AND OFFICERS ARE PROHIBITED

Generally, it will be unlawful under Sarbanes-Oxley for companies to make, extend, or renew credit in the form of personal loans to any director or officer, with limited exceptions.

REAL TIME DISCLOSURES OF IMPORTANT CHANGES

Sarbanes-Oxley contains a rule that requires companies to disclose to the public "on a rapid and current basis" and in "plain English," important changes in the financial condition or operations of the company with the purpose of protecting investors.

SUMMARY

The Sarbanes-Oxley Act, related regulations from the SEC, and the revised rules from the stock exchanges attempt to address the abuses perpetrated in recent business scandals. The new rules and regulations focus primarily on the following: independence of directors, particularly those dealing with the audit, compensation, and nominating processes; the expertise and procedures required to produce accurate financial statements; the need for full, accurate, and timely disclosure of financial results; and disclosures of trading that make it more difficult for directors and officers to profit from inside information. Moreover, the revised standards establish that the directors are responsible for ensuring that controls are in place to monitor behaviors within the organization and employees who observe fraudulent activities can report them without risk.

The effect of these laws and regulations has included increased attention by directors and management to the responsibilities with which they are charged. The new laws and regulations, in effect, codify what have been for some time the best practices at many organizations, and force all public corporations to adopt such practices, leveling the fields on which they compete.

The obvious weakness with laws is that legislation guarantees neither morality nor competence. Enforcement and compliance can be costly, and worries abound that heightened standards, personal responsibility, increased restrictions and penalties, and broader sanctions might keep talented and ethical individuals from accepting positions as officers and directors on boards of public companies. This concern is a valid one for U.S. corporations, as in the end, the success of a business is dependent on the competence of management and directors who are also honest and forthright in fulfilling their duties to the investors and other stakeholders.

Laws provide benefits, however, in setting standards for all public companies regarding the governing of their affairs and their dealings with investors. Sarbanes-Oxley has increased transparency and reduced the risk of corporate fraud by making it more difficult for the dishonest to hide their acts and mislead the public and by increasing the penalties for doing so. Accountability has taken on new meaning in most public companies, and both directors and officers have enhanced roles in financial reporting, disclosure, and controls.

One would expect that, over time, the new standards set by the Sarbanes-Oxley Act of 2002 and the revised rules of the NYSE and NASDAQ would improve not only the reporting of financial results, but also the results themselves, as they compel attendant changes in the operations, management, controls, and governance of publicly traded companies. Of equal importance, legislators, regulators, and compliant directors and executives hope to see the sought-after, associated restoration of public trust and confidence in corporate responsibility and financial reporting. It will take some time, though, before fair assessment may be made of these and other consequences of the revised rules and legislation.

CHAPTER 9

HOW DIRECTORS AND BOARDS GET INTO TROUBLE

INTRODUCTION

A review of the popular press reveals that corporate directors occasionally get into trouble. There are numerous definitions of trouble, with some forms occurring more frequently than others. Notable varieties of trouble occur when the corporation does not produce acceptable results, perhaps placing it in financial jeopardy, or violates the civil or criminal code and is sued or prosecuted. Directors can get into trouble for individual actions, and they can also get into trouble as a group. They can get into as much trouble from the things they did not do but should have done as from having done things they should not have done. The most all-encompassing definition would be that the company failed to achieve its goals. Trouble can also include the company and the board simply getting into contentious, controversial, or inconvenient situations.

What makes being a director even more perilous is that often it is not what one has or has not done as much as how things have worked out that determines the way a situation is evaluated. This implies that a particular course of action might be deemed acceptable at one point in time and wrong at another, depending on the accompanying circumstances. As the nature of the business and the relevant issues evolve over time, the knowledge and experience necessary for board service also change. Thus, once-competent directors can become less so as a result of changes in the environment.

The causes of trouble break into two broad categorizations, *incompetence* (that normally can lead to civil penalties) and *dishonesty* (that frequently can lead to criminal penalties). While the criminal penalties are the more dramatic, the civil actions are much more commonplace. Across the spectrum, a great deal more money is lost through incompetence than through criminal wrongdoing, especially when the cost of lost opportunities is considered.

AVOIDING A BAD SITUATION

The first reason directors get into trouble is that they allow themselves to be drawn into unfortunate situations. Directors may be motivated to join a board for a variety of reasons, including friendships, potential economic gain, networking, learning and exposure, and enhanced prestige. All of these can be valid reasons for joining a board in appropriate situations. Unless the potential director can carry out effective due diligence or knows the CEO, other directors, and situation well, any of these motives can also lead to a bad situation.

Whether we use the term bad, poor, or unfortunate, we mean, at a minimum, the difficult situation might involve substantial amounts of time, stress, and unpleasantness. If the business fails, it can cost a new director money and reputation. If the CEO or other directors are dishonest or unethical, a director can unwittingly be drawn into legal problems.

Thus, it is essential for those considering becoming a director to know the company and situation they are joining, and to be certain that they have the time and experience to assume the role and fulfill its responsibilities. If the other directors or the CEO have specific expectations, they should clearly state them before any new director joins the board.

INDIVIDUAL PROBLEMS

A director always should act with integrity. It should go without saying that blatantly dishonest behavior, such as stealing and outright lying, is universally frowned upon. Much unethical behavior, however, is excused with a "business is business" attitude. Because of this dichotomy, it is not always easy to determine when and where one crosses the line from behavior appropriate for a good, tough businessperson to that of an unethical opportunist and eventually to that of a dishonest scoundrel.

A variety of circumstances contribute to individual directors getting into trouble. Several of these are discussed below.

IGNORANCE

A major source of potential trouble for a director is a lack of understanding of the responsibilities and duties of being a director in a specific organization. Basic knowledge of these issues requires that directors understand the applicable laws and the organization's articles of incorporation and bylaws. It also implies that directors have at least a working understanding of the business and the industry in which it competes. As we have noted, ignorance offers no protection from prosecution or civil suit for directors who are nonetheless well intentioned.

LACK OF INDEPENDENCE

Lack of independence can be another source of problems for directors. If a director is personally or professionally close to the CEO or other directors, he or she will likely find it much more difficult to render objective judgments about important issues. Similarly, directors might be less likely to act independently if they are receiving substantial financial compensation or other benefits for serving as a director or for acting in a consulting role. A lack of independence becomes particularly important when things are not going well and the board must make difficult decisions, especially about the CEO and his or her proposals.

Directors must remain mindful of their fiduciary duty to represent the best interests of the shareholders, which requires independent thought and action.

CONFLICTS OF INTEREST

Conflicts of interest arise when a director has the potential to profit or benefit from a decision or action at the expense of the shareholders. Directors must avoid such situations, both in fact and appearance. The most common conflicts of interest arise from direct transactions with the business, competing in some way with the business, or using inside knowledge to seize a corporate opportunity away from the business.

The best way to deal with conflicts of interest is first to avoid them. If a conflict exists, full disclosure must be made and the director must abstain from any board actions involving the conflicted situation.

FAILURE TO EXECUTE THE DUTY OF CARE

Failure to execute the duty of care can be a major source of problems for busy directors. A director must stay informed about the business in general and about any particular issue being discussed or acted upon. If issues are complex, staying appropriately informed can take substantial time. If the issue requires knowledge or expertise beyond that of a director, he or she is entitled to rely on the representations and advice of management or other experts.

Judgment is required in determining when a director knows enough to make an informed decision. It begins with the level of confidence each director has in the CEO, management, and any experts employed. This confidence should not be placed blindly, but rather critically. As information is presented to the board, it must make sense to the directors, and they must think they understand enough about an issue to make an informed decision. If they do not feel this way, they must be persistent in asking probing questions or seeking additional input until satisfied.

The courts look at process in determining whether the duty of care has been met. The process should show the presentation of the facts and a full deliberation by the board of the issue under discussion. Maintaining records in the form of memoranda and minutes is vitally important in such circumstances.

STOCK-TRADING VIOLATIONS

A potential source of serious problems for directors of publicly owned corporations is any form of insider trading. Directors generally are deemed to have inside information not available to the public and are not permitted to trade on this information. Consequently, directors must strictly adhere to rules relating to when trading in a company's stock by directors is permitted. The rules stipulate blackout periods prior to quarterly earnings announcements or when some material transaction or action is being considered or announced. To be prudent, directors should buy or sell company stock only with the knowledge and approval of corporate counsel.

In addition to being prohibited from trading on inside information, directors may not disclose inside information to other parties who then make transactions in the stock. Recipients of inside information immediately become insiders themselves, and like directors, are barred from acting on the information by trading in the company's stock. The penalties for insider trading can be quite severe.

There are additional laws addressing trading limitations and reporting requirements of which directors should be aware. As we have noted, ignorance offers directors no protection.

COLLECTIVE BOARD PROBLEMS

While individual directors can get into trouble, the ways in which the board functions as a whole determine the long-term potential for problems. Board problems include:

- Poor business performance that brings about the wrath of shareholders
- Lack of board leadership
- Inadequate or inappropriate involvement in management

- Entrenchment
- Internal political or personal conflicts
- Ineffective board organization and processes
- Securities violations
- Conspiring in or tolerating legal violations

Each of these concerns is addressed below.

POOR BUSINESS PERFORMANCE THAT BRINGS ABOUT THE WRATH OF SHAREHOLDERS

Consistently poor company performance over a long period of time is a familiar source of major board problems. Extended poor performance very often indicates that a company's board is not getting its job done effectively. Exhibit 9-1 reports the results of a review of the financial performance over the following five years of two groups of 25 companies designated as having the best and worst boards of directors by *Business Week* in late 1996. The results are interesting, although they scarcely could be considered conclusive regarding the relationship between apparent board effectiveness and company performance. Still, we can say with certainty that board decisions and actions (or lack of action) affect a firm's operations, and consequently its results.

As noted previously, a fundamental decision of a board is selecting the business or businesses in which the firm will engage. The businesses selected should be advantageous ones for which the company has, or can get, the resources and competencies to compete effectively. If the company is engaged in businesses that are not attractive, or in which it cannot be competitive, it should determine how to exit those businesses.

	Under-performed the S&P 500	Performed with the S&P 500 (+/-10% Cumulative Return)	Outperformed the S&P 500	No Longer Exist
Worst Boards	12	1	4	8
Best Boards	6	4	12	3

Common stock performance: May 20, 1997 – May 20, 2002.
Companies are from lists in *BusinessWeek*, November 26, 1996. Stock performance was measured from May 20, 1997 to May 20, 2002 from public sources.

EXHIBIT 9-1   Performance of 25 Best and 25 Worst Boards—May 1997–May 2002

When a company's operating results are not strong, a decline in the stock price is an early sign of shareholder dissatisfaction. This situation can escalate into the formation of dissident groups of shareholders, sometimes ending in proxy fights to replace the board or in hostile takeover attempts, or both.

Companies produce poor financial results for a wide range of reasons. Those over which the board has influence or control include being in the wrong business, hiring a weak CEO, or failing to have an effective strategy. Even with a desirable business and a competent CEO, the board must remain engaged in carrying out its duties. A number of other problems boards encounter as a body are discussed below.

LACK OF BOARD LEADERSHIP

Most of the mistakes boards make result from ineffective board leadership. Probably the most common form of poor leadership is for a company to have a combined chairman/CEO who dominates the board. If the CEO is also chairman, to whom does the CEO report? In this situation the CEO reports to a board of which he or she is chairman. The potential problems with this situation are obvious.

A solution is to divide the chairman and CEO roles into the two jobs they represent. The chairman then becomes the leader of the board. If the jobs are combined, a sometimes satisfactory alternative is to have a formally appointed lead director, who may be the chairman of the committee of outside directors. He or she performs the same roles as a nonemployee chairman, except that he or she does not preside at board meetings.

The responsibilities of the chairman or lead outside director include working closely with the CEO to determine board agendas, working with the nominating committee to organize the board committees, managing the board's deliberative processes, and serving as liaison between the board and the CEO.

Another level of board leadership comes from the committee chairpersons, who perform these same roles for each standing committee. A third level of leadership often moves among the directors during discussions and depends on the topic and the directors' levels of expertise.

Overall, the leadership of the board should ensure that the board constructively addresses important issues in a timely and efficient manner, and that any conflict among members is appropriately resolved. Consider the potential for a board to fall into a troubled situation when the power to set the agenda is in the hands of a weak CEO or when the leader of the nominating committee fails to implement a process to find properly qualified directors. Strong board leadership at all levels is required for sustained success.

INADEQUATE OR INAPPROPRIATE INVOLVEMENT IN MANAGEMENT

Determining the distinction between the board's responsibilities and those of management is a balancing act for directors. Dangers arise when a board delegates authority for action without effective oversight. In such cases the board effectively abdicates its responsibilities. At the other end of the spectrum, the board should not micromanage the affairs of the business. If the board is too involved in the details of the business, it is very difficult to hold management accountable. Board members who prefer to be in control, for example those who have or continue to run their own businesses, often find it difficult to give up control to the CEO.

ENTRENCHMENT

Entrenchment is another common symptom of ineffective boards. Entrenchment occurs when a high percentage of members remain on the board for too long. Frequently with entrenched boards, the directors no longer are willing or able to proactively address the issues confronting the business. Perhaps they are too close to a long-term CEO to be independent, or the nature of the business has changed to the point that they no longer have the skills and experience to be effective. In some cases, entrenched board members simply have become tired or too complacent.

As noted in Chapter 3, some observers advocate term limits as a means to avoid entrenchment, and, in theory, this would seem reasonable. Term limits work reasonably well in many not-for-profit organizations, but they have certain obvious shortcomings for the public corporation today. Term limits based on age are helpful, as are rules requiring that members submit their resignations when their employment status changes. The resignations might not be accepted, but the situation is automatically reviewed and a graceful exit becomes available.

A more effective way of avoiding entrenchment is to develop a good process of board evaluation and a culture that is willing to rotate members off the board if they become ineffective. Such a process might be difficult to bring about, but strong boards find a way.

INTERNAL POLITICAL OR PERSONAL CONFLICTS

Board work requires a team effort. When members of the team do not get along or are not capable of collaboration, a board's functioning suffers. Sometimes matters of personality or style cause problems. Some very bright and successful people simply do not function well in groups, especially when they want to be in control. These apparently highly capable individuals might find compromising to reach a consensus or being overruled very difficult personally.

Boards might also suffer from personality conflicts among certain members or political struggles intended to enhance control within the board. Conflicting goals for the organization might also create conflict among board members. For instance, one director might believe that seeking a short-term profit from exiting a business is a preferable strategy, while another might believe it is best to build the business for the long run.

Regardless of the reason, conflicts among directors complicate what is already a challenging job. When carried to an extreme, such conflicts can get a board in trouble for a number of reasons. Dissatisfied directors might resign and create negative publicity. Some might even go so far as to wage a proxy fight against the proclaimed position of the CEO. Others might bully the majority to make poor decisions. Finally, a torn board might be so factionalized that it fails to act when it should.

INEFFECTIVE BOARD ORGANIZATION AND PROCESSES

Boards that fail to build effective leadership and committee structures are not likely to be very successful. Likewise, those that do not follow good processes in their deliberations and decision making are apt to make mistakes. A great deal of thought should be given to the organization and the processes required to enhance the likelihood of effective operations. In some states, following an appropriate process is what is deemed essential to meeting the duties of director, not necessarily the substance, reasonableness, or even rationality of a board's decision.

SECURITIES VIOLATIONS

Group securities violations traditionally have evolved from ineffective information disclosures, while individual violations have tended to be about insider trading. The new Sarbanes-Oxley legislation expands the requirements for the way a board functions, particularly with regard to independence and internal controls.

CONSPIRING IN OR TOLERATING LEGAL VIOLATIONS

A board that conspires to break the law is very likely to get into serious trouble. The results of such situations are obvious, as all involved parties suffer the unfortunate consequences. Directors must have the strength of character to respond to any pressures that hint of legal wrongdoing.

Furthermore, they should immediately act to protect themselves and the interests of the shareholders from those with criminal intent.

CONCLUSIONS

We recognize that the foundation of American business was established on the notion of capable people doing an honest job. This foundation to a large degree remains, although perhaps with the amendment of capable people doing an honest job within the law. In response to scandals that plunged corporate giants to the brink of bankruptcy with startling speed, laws have been passed and rules tightened to protect investors as well as honest business people from the transgressions of the dishonest among them.

Our entire economic system, the most productive and wealth-creating in history, is vulnerable and at risk if effective governance practices are not in place across the broad spectrum of publicly held companies. Lacking widespread effective governance, capital markets will operate inefficiently in an atmosphere of distrust and with continued erosion of investor confidence. Without public access to these markets, economic growth and our rising standard of living will undoubtedly falter.

This economic base cannot continue in the absence of effective governance practices. We cannot rely exclusively on new and ever more restrictive legislation or on the various regulatory agencies to eliminate corporate malfeasance through more stringent enforcement of existing and new regulations, necessary as these are. Looking ahead, we are convinced that companies must transform their boards into effective instruments of sound governance to ensure a productive economy. Acquiring and perpetuating an independent and competent board of directors must become a primary goal of every publicly held corporation.

Morality and ethics cannot be legislated or even mandated, as history has proven time and again. Furthermore, there are many ways directors and boards can find themselves in trouble without violating the law. Ultimately, the burden for responsible and effective governance will fall on existing boards and the integrity of their nominating processes, for it is through these processes that the boards of tomorrow will be selected.

We salute the thousands of directors who struggle to make our system perform. We remain hopeful that they and the directors of tomorrow will ever strive for continuous improvement in performing their essential duties on behalf of all of their companies' stakeholders.

INDEX

Adelphia, 1
agenda for board meeting, **45–46**
annual meeting of shareholders, 33
Arthur Andersen, 1
articles of incorporation, legal
    obligations of directors and, 9
audit committee, 39–40
    independent auditors and,
        influencing of, 83
    regulatory issues and, responsibility
        under, 81–82

base salary, compensating CEOs, **62,
    63**
board of directors, 3–4
    character and integrity of board
        members in, 27
    characteristics necessary in board
        members, 27–28
    commitment of board members in, 27
    due diligence in, 26–27
    election of directors in, 29
    expertise requirements in, 25–26
    getting and keeping, 19–30
    governance committee and, selection
        of new members in, 23–24
    group effectiveness in members of,
        27–28
    indemnification of, 16
    independence in, inside vs. outside
        directors, 24–25, 80–81, 89
    lawyers, consultants, customers,
        suppliers on, 25

board of directors (*Cont.*):
    legal obligations of, 7–17. See also
        legal obligations of directors
    maintaining effectiveness of board
        and, 29–30
    major shareholders on, 25
    management role of. See management
        and board
    mutual agreement of all parties in
        selection and, 28
    nominee's decision to serve and, 28–29
    openings in board, number of, 24
    organization of, 31–46. See organiza-
        tion of board
    profile for board in, 24–26
    proxy contests and, 29
    recruitment process in, 26–27
    retired CEOs and executives on, 25
    search and selection process in, 26, **26**
    selection of, CEO as selector, 22–23
    size of, 20–21
    terms of directors in, 21–22
    "business judgment rule," legal obliga-
        tions of directors and, 14
business knowledge of directors, 70–72
business performance problems, 91–92,
    91
bylaws, 31–33
    changing, as defensive measure, 35
    legal obligations of directors and, 9

capitalism, 2
care, duty of, 11–12, 14–15, 89–90

Note: **Boldface** numbers indicate illustrations.

97

About the Authors

John L. Colley, Jr. is a professor, **Jacqueline L. Doyle** is a visiting assistant professor, **George W. Logan** is a visiting lecturer, and **Wallace Stettinius** is a visiting lecturer at the University of Virginia's Darden Graduate School of Business Administration.